RESEARCH LIBRARIES AND TECHNOLOGY

A Report to the Sloan Foundation

HERMAN H. FUSSLER

THE UNIVERSITY OF CHICAGO PRESS
CHICAGO and LONDON

THE UNIVERSITY OF CHICAGO STUDIES IN LIBRARY SCIENCE
Published under the auspices of
THE LIBRARY QUARTERLY

THE UNIVERSITY OF CHICAGO PRESS, CHICAGO 60637
THE UNIVERSITY OF CHICAGO PRESS, LTD., LONDON

© 1973 by The University of Chicago. All rights reserved
Published 1973
Printed in the United States of America

International Standard Book Number: 0-226-27558-2 (clothbound)
Library of Congress Catalog Card Number: 73-81481

THE UNIVERSITY OF CHICAGO STUDIES IN LIBRARY SCIENCE

RESEARCH LIBRARIES
AND TECHNOLOGY

CONTENTS

Foreword vii

Preface ix

1. Libraries and Technology from Several Perspectives 1
2. Some Current Aspects of the Large University Library 12
3. Bibliographical and Library Processing Functions 26
4. Shared Resources, Photocopying, and Facsimile Transmission . . . 33
5. The Computer and the Library 51
6. Examples of Computer Applications in Library Operations and Information Access 62
7. Some General Observations and Conclusions 73

References 81

Acknowledgments 85

Index 87

FOREWORD

In December 1970 the Sloan Foundation established a program in educational technology. As an aid to the development of this program, the Foundation has commissioned several state-of-the-art studies in particular technologies. One such study was this report on library technology, done for us by Dr. Herman H. Fussler of the University of Chicago. Although Dr. Fussler's original report was an internal document at the Foundation, we found it so helpful in giving us a grasp of the field and so broad in its implications as to deserve general circulation. Our view of its importance was reinforced by the comments of a number of heads of research libraries to whom the report was sent. The Foundation is therefore glad to make Dr. Fussler's excellent report available to a wider audience.

NILS Y. WESSEL, President
The Alfred P. Sloan Foundation

PREFACE

The general origins of this report are stated in the Foreword. It should be noted that the report was drafted in an effort to respond to the presumed needs of a distinguished advisory group established by the Sloan Foundation to examine a broad range of problems and potentials associated with educational technology. Since the report was not addressed to librarians, and since technology and libraries are both means to ends, it seemed important to try to relate technological potentials and limitations to at least some of the major current trends, problems, and objectives of the library. Such an approach seems essential if suitable policy and priority issues are to be identified and implemented. I concluded that it was also essential to deal with several nontechnological measures that may be fully as significant as technology in effecting advantageous changes in some of the functions which libraries attempt to provide.

The focus of the report is primarily upon the problems of the large, university, research-oriented library. It is here that one finds the most difficult resource-access and bibliographical control[1] problems. If one can significantly improve both of these operations for the large, research-oriented institutions, there are likely to be direct or indirect benefits for the smaller library, while the reverse situation is much less likely.

The extremely rapid rate of technological change, and the rather wide span of potential technologies that are relevant to library operations and information access, make time and scale-of-operation predictions and the related systems design specifications hazardous. Since one can, more or less comfortably, assume that "almost anything" is technologically possible if one sets the time sufficiently far forward—or is willing to be either casual or optimistic about costs—I have attempted to focus on possible changes or developments for the more immediate future, that is, for the present and the next five to ten years. In such planning there are serious risks of planning in too small and trivial a manner, or of making developmental or operational investments that may become technologically obsolete before they can be seriously implemented, or of planning without regard to longer-term evolutionary capabilities in terms of emerging technologies or users' needs. The

---

[1] "Bibliographical control" in this report refers, unless indicated otherwise, to the full range of bibliographical apparatus or tools by means of which a reader or library staff member, may learn of relevant materials and the physical location of cited documents; e.g., author, title, subject, and classified catalogs whether in card, printed-book, computer-display, or other forms; abstracting and indexing services; citation indexes; lists of serial titles; union catalogs; lists of dissertations; etc.

effort to avoid each of these risks deserves very serious attention in the research library environment.

I assume that basically technology should be used where it can improve the cost/benefit or cost/effectiveness ratios of existing processes or services, or where it can extend or provide essentially new or improved services that society is willing to support. It is quite clear that at the present time relevant technologies are available that are not fully exploited. The principal reasons for nonexploitation are primarily, but not entirely, related to economic, conceptual, bibliographical, and organizational, rather than technological, problems. However, there are still some difficult technical problems.

The general objectives of the large research library are, in effect, open-ended and cover an extremely wide range of actual or potential requirements. Satisfactory techniques for economic analysis of the benefits of access to recorded knowledge or information are conspicuously lacking. Yet it is evident that our society, our research programs, and our educational systems are critically dependent upon reasonably efficient access to literature and information. However, much of the scholarly and educational access to information is normally provided to the user outside a marketplace economy. This makes it difficult to develop new or improved information- or literature-access systems with the assurance that such systems can be justified and supported.

Even so, the long-term, most effective utilizations of technology are likely to be the result of careful analyses of requirements and fairly large-scale systems approaches. One may also achieve some independent improvements in the efficiency of various local library operations or processing functions. However, the basic economic and other characteristics of large research libraries and the characteristics of the relevant technologies are such that entirely local, independent, technological, developmental endeavors are unlikely to save large sums of money or radically improve performance within the limits of existing expenditure levels and concepts of service. This is especially true if technological developmental costs are included as a part of the long-term service costs. For these reasons it seems likely to be most beneficial if technology and other alternatives can be utilized in ways that will be of benefit to many institutions. There appear to be a number of ways in which this can be accomplished.

In choosing new or modified information- or library-systems designs there tend to be conflicts between the priorities to be given to cost-efficiency objectives and performance objectives. It is evident that choices or priorities in these areas may, unless one is very careful, lead to different and incompatible solutions. The elusiveness of cost/benefit data in relation to information access is not a barrier to the development of new capabilities, but it does make the justification for such capabilities more difficult.

The report is organized in the following manner. In Chapter 1, essentially as a means of orientation, a number, but certainly not all, of the major studies of libraries and technology that have appeared in the past decade are summarized in a very synoptic fashion. The chapter concludes with a number of general observations and conclusions that have tended to shape much of the balance of the report.

In the second chapter, instead of technology, attention is given to some data on library cost trends, the relationships between library costs and total institutional costs, rates of library growth, the frequency of use of certain categories of library materials, and several related matters. These kinds of data are, in general, quite familiar to librarians; they may be less familiar to academic administrators and planners. Such data deserve attention because they rather sharply illuminate what seem to be some serious basic problems or trends in the current or future operations of the larger research libraries. There are a variety of direct implications for the use of technology and other alternatives.

Chapter 3 is concerned with some of the characteristics, problems, and opportunities for change in the basic apparatus for bibliographical control.

The relentless pressures to expand the depth and scope of large research collections are well known. Many observers have suggested that relief from these pressures may be supplied by technology. In Chapter 4 three widely discussed methods for extending resource availability and reducing the pressures on local collection growth are discussed: shared resource systems, microforms and other photocopies, and the facsimile transmission of textual materials. The role of the computer in library operations is reviewed in a general way in Chapter 5, while Chapter 6 outlines, very briefly, a variety of current applications of computers and closely related technologies. In the final chapter I have attempted to restate a number of general observations and conclusions.

1

LIBRARIES AND TECHNOLOGY FROM SEVERAL PERSPECTIVES

An analysis of library operations in relationship to technology is not made particularly easy by the voluminous literature that now exists on the subject. Some impression of the range and diversity of the recent literature will be apparent by examining the articles and bibliographies in Cuadra [17] and Becker [9] and the extensive bibliography compiled by Billingsley [10]. The cited literature tends to lack, in part for valid reasons, firm cost or objective performance data on both existing operations and on new applications of technology. It is sometimes even difficult to distinguish what has been accomplished from what is being contemplated. Conventional library operating data also tend to be inconsistent and unreliable for careful economic or performance analyses, and are related primarily to inputs rather than outputs.

However, there have been a number of major studies of many aspects of libraries in relation to technology by specialists with ample staffs and with ample time for investigation. Most of these studies have focused primarily upon the data-processing capabilities of computers. A very brief summary of some of these major surveys and conferences may be helpful as an introduction to some of the issues in the field.

THE LIBRARY OF CONGRESS STUDY (1963)[2]

One of the earliest large-scale studies of the application of computers and certain related technologies to library problems was summarized in the report *Automation and the Library of Congress* [3], published in 1963. On the basis of a preliminary investigation of current and projected costs and requirements at the Library of Congress, a survey team of specialists, under the chairmanship of Gilbert W. King, concluded that computer processing of bibliographic data, catalog searching, and document retrieval was technically feasible for large research libraries, and would actually prove superior to the then current manual methods on a cost/effectiveness basis. Furthermore, such computer processing would facilitate the development of a national library system and would eventually greatly improve the responsiveness of large research libraries to the requirements of their users. Accordingly, the team was enthusiastic in its recommendation that the Librarian of Congress undertake a detailed study of system specifications and, on the completion of that study, request funds for the implementation of the system. On the basis

---

[2]The dates shown in this section of the report are publication dates; they may be as much as one or two years after the basic study period itself.

of the preliminary analysis, automation of a network of research libraries, the central node being the Library of Congress, would require an estimated $50-$70 million. The development was recommended primarily in terms of anticipated response and service benefits, rather than for any savings in operating costs or improvements in cost/effectiveness ratios. The committee concluded that the retrieval of the "intellectual content" of books by automatic methods was not then feasible for large collections.

THE LIBRARY OF CONGRESS-AIRLIE CONFERENCE (1964)

The importance of a detailed library systems study was recognized by the King Committee. The fact that such an analysis should be independent of particular designs for implementation was recognized and elaborated upon by Swanson, at a conference on library automation sponsored by the Library of Congress in 1963 [51]. A clear and formal specification of library purposes and requirements would serve a dual purpose. First, such an analysis would permit rational cost/effectiveness comparisons between competing systems. Second, and equally important, with a formal statement of library requirements, systems engineers could proceed to design hardware and software systems specifically for library use, possibly at costs well within the range of library budgets.

A point of view fundamentally opposed to that laid down by Swanson was also apparent in this and succeeding conferences. While Swanson would first ask, "What are the purposes, or the requirements of the library system in question?" and only after answering this query proceed to investigate the best means to achieve those objectives, the approach taken by many librarians and other specialists was the reverse. This approach is characterized by an a priori decision to "automate." The query then asked was, "Which of the new technologies can best be applied toward the accomplishment of the 'automation' goal?" Much of the literature of library automation is thus concerned with examining the capabilities of existing and future technologies, often to the exclusion of careful analyses of library or user requirements.

THE INTREX CONFERENCE (1965)

The INTREX project at the Massachusetts Institute of Technology is perhaps a good example of the effort to exploit, insofar as possible, a large array of pertinent technologies in order to develop an experimental or prototype test system of information and literature access in the context of a relatively broad or general assessment of needs made by a diverse group of scientists, engineers, humanists, and others. At the Planning Conference in 1965 [43] the development of a model library was recommended, having such capabilities as automatic textual access, fact retrieval, and access to "the on-line intellectual community" via a network of libraries joined by time-shared computer systems. Mechanization of current library procedures would be accomplished "in the early stages" of the project. The issue of economic benefits or feasibility was not seriously discussed, though the question was raised. The assumption was that the benefits of such a system would be found sufficiently attractive to generate the necessary support.

THE SYSTEM DEVELOPMENT CORPORATION STUDIES (1967)(1969)

The System Development Corporation undertook two important studies dealing with technology and libraries. With these investigations the focus of major studies shifted somewhat away from automation or data processing within individual libraries toward the establishment of national systems, or networks, for information storage and dissemination. Underlying the System Development Corporation's recommendations and conclusions in the first of these studies [14] was the assumption that it is the responsibility of the federal government to ensure "that there exists within the United States at least one accessible copy of each significant publication of the worldwide scientific and technical literature." This report also includes a substantial survey of *fifteen* other major proposals for handling scientific and technical literature that had been published by 1966.

The second System Development Corporation study [53], conducted in 1967 and published in 1969, was directed less to science information systems and more to libraries and technology. The study identified three possible approaches for the improvement of the nation's libraries: (1) to make no attempt to accelerate the rate of improvement or radically to change present concepts of requirements and the means of achieving them; (2) systematically to plan and develop a highly integrated library system, national in scope; or (3) to identify and support selected projects of national scope and importance. The first of these approaches was considered inadequate in the face of rapidly increasing user needs. The second approach was not recommended because agreement on common goals was felt to be unlikely, because sources of funding would be uncertain, and because the sovereign state of individual libraries might make the management of such a system extraordinarily difficult. The third approach was recommended.

Five projects were singled out where "operational" systems could be achieved in from two to four years. These were to develop: (1) a prototype network of regional libraries, (2) an expanded, computer-based National Union Catalog, (3) a national bibliography, (4) a national referral and loan network, and (5) a national library storage and microform depository system. In addition, it was recommended that there be "a comprehensive program of technology-oriented library research, development, and education." Estimated costs for all five of the recommended projects amounted to $400–$500 million over a four-year period, over and above present funding from all sources. Supporting research and development would include systematic statements of library and user requirements, the development and standardization of library-oriented hardware and software, and both formal and on-the-job education and training of library administrative and technical personnel. Because all of the recommended projects were national in scope, a permanent body, public, private, or federal, would need to be created to take responsibility for planning, developing, coordinating, and implementing the recommended projects. Among the proposed functions for the administrative body were the development of federal policies in matters relating to libraries, including the education of librarians, copyright legislation, and the operation of government depository libraries; the development of minimal standards for federally related activities; and the development of cost and budgetary guidelines.

THE SATCOM REPORT (1969)

In two other studies the need for a cohesive national program was perceived and the establishment of a coordinating body recommended.

The Committee on Scientific and Technical Communication of the National Academy of Sciences (SATCOM) reached some fifty-five specific conclusions and recommendations [39]. Among them were the following: (1) A joint commission on scientific and technical communication should be created, responsible to the councils of the National Academy of Sciences and the National Academy of Engineering, the general purpose of which would be to foster coordination, cooperation, and shared responsibility within the scientific community and between the government and private organizations. (2) A federal commission should be established to study problems of copyright in depth, especially as they relate to new technologies. (3) The major responsibility for the identification of user needs belongs to the scientific and technical societies. (4) The expansion of the activities of *consolidation* (the writing of review articles) and *reprocessing* (the production of specialized bibliographies and indexes from existing indexing and abstracting services) is the most pressing short-run need for effective scientific information transfer. (5) In recognition of the fact that uncommunicated research is of little value, the departments and agencies of the federal government which are engaged in sponsoring research should fund the literature-access services required for the communication of literature to the scientific community. (6) Funding policy with respect to grants to research libraries should be aimed at introducing more realistic cost analysis, a closer relationship between costs and services, and more options of extra services to be paid for by the recipient. (7) More attention should be given to principles of operations research in the analysis of library services.

THE CONFERENCE ON IMAGE STORAGE AND TRANSMISSION (1970)

At another conference [26], it was made abundantly clear—if it was not already—that technology existed capable of revolutionizing traditional methods of storing, retrieving, and transmitting information. Only just alluded to, however, were some of the problems involved in making such a transformation. Those identified included the following: (1) there is little standardization in equipment and materials; (2) it is not clear how the needs of users can be measured; (3) it is not clear how one can best measure the effectiveness of various systems; and (4) thus it is not clear how one can relate the costs of various systems to their effectiveness.

It was generally true in this period that rather futuristic and simplistic views were taken of the "automation" process, by librarians, technologists, and systems specialists alike. Many of the major studies were directed primarily to the literature and informational needs of science and technology. Enthusiasm and optimism ran high, while some of the basic problems were essentially ignored or grossly underestimated.

THE "WIGINGTON" REPORT (1971)

In one of the most recent major reports [40], the Information Systems Panel of the Computer Science and Engineering Board of the National Academy of Sciences, under the chairmanship of Ronald L. Wigington, recommended greater involvement of science policy makers in the analysis and planning of information systems, better operational data on actual library services, the development of a prototype pilot system of sufficient size and generality to lead to sound long-term planning, the critical study of information networks, the development of suitable software systems for managing very large files, improvements in the size and cost of very large digital storage capacity, studies of the economics and other characteristics of communications-based systems versus local systems, and procedures to ensure that all bibliographical and indexing data are available to all libraries in computer form. The panel also recommended that greater use of computer-controlled text in microform be carefully developed, that libraries have the capacity to provide access to machine-readable factual data as well as bibliographical data, and that further training and educational opportunities be made available to key workers and managers.

THE CONFERENCE ON INTERLIBRARY COMMUNICATIONS AND INFORMATION NETWORKS (1971)

The editor of the proceedings of this conference [9] summarized some of its conclusions in the following words:

> A national network of libraries and information-centers appears to be a viable and attractive concept; . . . the individual is the one who will be served by a national network; . . . the development of the network concept is an interdisciplinary task; . . . social engineering is required to overcome many of the obstacles to network progress. There seems little doubt that technology can aid the process, but the fundamental requirement is to motivate

institutions to develop new patterns of organization that will permit consortia and networks to operate effectively. Conference discussions made it very clear that a monolithic network structure imposed from the top down will not work.

The working groups at this conference came to a variety of other basic conclusions about the relationships of networks to the current state of technology, the acute need for greater standardization in bibliographical data, the need for access to more comprehensive bibliographical data bases, the importance of cost analyses, the need to solve some important technological problems in data transfer, and a variety of other matters. The conference participants seemingly did not attempt to specify precise functions for the proposed networks. However, the "Working Group on Network Needs and Development," in its summary, provided the following: "It is essential that networking develop out of the existing system. A national effort (1) should be a composite of many efforts and systems, (2) should be based on successful experience, (3) should continue to be increasingly personal, (4) should extend the choices available to individuals, (5) should be responsive to change, and (6) must work."

THE CONFERENCE BOARD REPORT ON INFORMATION TECHNOLOGY (1972)

This major study [16] departs in a number of respects from those previously cited. It is concerned with the entire spectrum of information technology, envisaged as a "new resource of strategic national and international importance" involving the "collection, storage, processing, dissemination, and use of information." The expectations as to effective dates for major extensions of existing capabilities, or the development of entirely new ones, extend from the early 1980s to the end of the century. The general conclusion of the report is that that there now are or shortly will be, very powerful information and communication technologies that, if properly used, could quite profoundly affect the means as well as the quality of access to information. In this respect the study resembles in some ways, and goes beyond in others, some of the observations and conclusions of Kemeny [29] and Licklider [32]. The organizational, planning, and policy problems are perceived as quite difficult.

The section of the study that deals with education contains the following observations on the academic library:

> Although the library is an important status symbol and an essential resource for a university, the fact is that, today, it plays a subsidiary role in the educational process. Only a small fraction of students use library facilities much. One reason is the gap between the growing volume of published information and the antiquated techniques employed for its storage and retrieval. The time and effort involved in using a library are frequently excessive for the value obtained. The strong pressures for library automation have had few visible results so far. This situation is likely

to change within the coming decade, as cost-effective solutions to the problem of convenient access to stored information start to appear, with the result that *the library of the 1980's may be radically different in structure and function from today's library* [italics in original].... It is likely to be important as a repository and distribution center of recorded presentations in cassette or equivalent form, on a limitless variety of subjects.... Progress in information storage and retrieval technology is certain to make obsolete the concept of the catalog and the book stack as we know them today.... A nationwide computerized network is likely to become a reality in the 1980's. If the cost of communicating data declines by a factor of ten as it is expected to do by the beginning of the next decade, it may be economically feasible to centralize the storage of books, periodicals, etc., in a few convenient locations, thus greatly reducing the heavy burden of storing printed information under the present system, while at the same time greatly increasing the range and variety of information conveniently available to the user. [16, pp. 116–17]

The study deals with a variety of other pertinent issues, for example, "Can Information Technology Be Managed?" "Information Technology: Power without Design, Thrust without Direction," and "The Changing Information Environment: A Selective Typography."

SUMMARY

In addition to the cited studies and conferences there are, of course, a substantial number of major studies on various disciplinary information systems or needs, for instance, medicine, chemistry, physics, psychology, and the behavioral and biological sciences. There is also a large body of literature reporting on various efforts or proposals to apply technology to specific institutional or disciplinary situations in the United States, Canada, Great Britain, and Europe. There is a distinctly smaller body of literature dealing with information-access theories, with the economics of information or literature access and its values, and with long-term library planning that realistically projects the consequences, priorities, and alternatives of various possible courses of action. There is, of course, a very large body of technical literature on computers, data storage techniques, programming, communication technologies, photographic reproduction, and related areas of interest.

The cited studies, and those closely related to them, are too large and too diverse to offer easy summary conclusions, but a few observations seem possible.

1. There appears to be a very strong consensus that some technologies are presently relevant to information and literature access and to library operations. There seems to be less agreement on priorities, the scale or levels of application, and the most suitable strategies for bringing about major changes or improvements.

2. In these studies the primary rationale for the recommended changes seems to be related to the need for sharp improvements in the responsiveness of library and information-access systems. Net, overall cost reductions, or cost stabilization, if in prospect, seem to have been given a somewhat lower priority in most of the cited studies. However, the expectation of substantially improved cost/effectiveness ratios *is* stated or strongly implied in virtually all of these reports.

3. The capital investment required to bring about a reasonably rapid, large-scale alteration of existing information and library-access systems is not stated in a number of the reports. Where stated, as in the System Development Corporation study [53], or in the King report on the automation of the Library of Congress [3], the amounts seem substantial. However, when examined in terms of total aggregate library expenditures,[3] cancer research, space flights, a nuclear-powered submarine, or a variety of other expenditures, the amounts seem relatively small. Furthermore there are some ominous library trends and fiscal support problems that may result in the assignment of greater values to technology in relation to ultimate cost stabilization—if not reduction.

4. As the "Wigington" report [40] indicates: "The primary bar to development of national computer-based library and information systems is no longer basically a technology-feasibility problem. Rather it is the combination of complex institutional and organizational human-related problems and the inadequate economic/value system associated with these activities." These problems have not been solved. No strong national mechanism for the effective analysis of needs, long-term systems planning, or implementation of new and larger systems of information/literature access has emerged. Indeed, too strong or authoritarian a mechanism would be unacceptable. Yet it is evident that some common, coherent services and functions, including planning, are needed to build a more effective national system of information and literature access. The Conference Board study on information technology asserts that this is likely to be a very serious problem for the entire information-access field [16, pp. 9–18].

5. There have also been technical, design, priority, and intellectual problems that have proved more intractable and difficult than was anticipated ten or so years ago.

6. It has become increasingly evident that successful, large-scale, computer software systems to handle complex data-access requirements cannot be developed independently by every large (or small) library or discipline-oriented professional society. There simply is not enough money, and the functional need for such extreme variation has not been demonstrated and is highly improbable.

---

[3]Aggregate expenditures for 2,500 college and university library expenditures in the United States came to $730 million in 1971–72 [12, p. 147]. The seventy-eight larger university libraries of the United States and Canada that belonged to the Association of Research Libraries reported 1971–72 expenditures totaling $260,515,000 in 1971–72.

7. It has been difficult to transfer existing capabilities from one computer or institutional environment to another, and some projects have been criticized because they were not "transferable." The criticism may be inappropriate if directed to some technical capabilities that are still being developed in prototype applications. There have been, of course, classical difficulties in the general transfer of reasonably high-efficiency software systems from one computer environment to another. There are now emerging a number of possible solutions to this problem.

8. Few, if any, of the large-scale, national, library-related system recommendations contained in these various reports have been carried out, though some large-scale literature- or data-oriented systems are now operational, for example, in medicine, chemistry, toxicology, and the Atomic Energy Commission.

9. It is probably reasonable to expect that the scholarly library and its staff will increasingly need to become a major point of access for factual data as well as bibliographical data and many other kinds of information. The classical concept of limiting the library's functions primarily to the selection, acquisition, organization, and servicing of a local collection of documents will not effectively meet the needs of an increasing number of users for either literature or data access.

10. There have been some important extensions in our general understanding of technical problems; some significant technological capabilities have been developed; some important progress has been made in developing standards for machine-based bibliographical data and in providing national access to such data; and many of the intellectual problems of organizing access to recorded information are becoming clearer.

11. Despite a few critical responses to technology, its alleged misuse, or its failure thus far to produce significant operating economies, the research library community has accepted, with varying degrees of knowledge or enthusiasm, the need for some basic changes in library procedures and operations, including more effective uses of technology. However, the view that there may need to be even more basic conceptual and operational changes in the ways that libraries function and provide access to recorded knowledge has perhaps not yet been generally accepted by either the library or the scholarly communities.

12. Some of the major reports on the current adequacy of disciplinary information access have pointed to rather severe deficiencies in the current literature control and related access systems (e.g. [14, 39, 41, 42, 44, 54]).

13. There has, in general, been a failure to prepare one or more general models through which the requirements and purposes of libraries or library-information networks could be more clearly and systematically specified and examined in terms of existing and alternative capabilities and designs. This need has been recognized in several committe reports and by several individuals as being of great importance. Most of the cited studies note the importance of careful library systems analyses, of determining more

precisely the extremely wide range of user needs, of recognizing the extreme variations in types of information and literature that must be made available, of developing schema to measure quantitatively the benefits derived from various systems and to compare the costs of new systems, and their stated benefits, with the costs and benefits of existing systems. There are serious gaps in theories of communication and information utilization. These matters are clearly difficult, but very important, as one examines the long-term potentials of technology and plans for new information- and literature-access systems.

14. Although it is not stressed in these reports, it is evident that technology is only one of many measures that need to be taken to improve access to literature and information. There are a variety of essentially nontechnological measures or changes that could equal or even exceed the immediate values of technology in the improvement of such access. A limited number of these alternatives are discussed in this report.

15. For those who may be disturbed by the prospects of technology, it may be worth noting that these studies rather strongly imply that the major improvements and changes sought can best be achieved in an evolutionary manner, that many basic library functions are critically important, and that these functions are very unlikely to be quickly or easily superseded by some simple—or even sophisticated—technology. However, it is equally essential to observe that there are also stated and implied criticisms of the library and its effectiveness that must be taken very seriously.

CONCLUSION

As Verner Clapp noted in the Foreword to Licklider's study [32]: "There is perhaps no question that makes more instant demand upon the combined experience and imagination of the respondents, or as a result, more widely differentiates one response from another, than does the question, 'How should one explore the library of the future?'"

We clearly have the means for bringing about some very large-scale and basic improvements in our concepts and methods of access to recorded knowledge and information. There are critical needs for such improvements, although it may not presently be possible to demonstrate the benefits of such changes in economic or other quantifiable ways. The achievements of such improvements will require money, improved organizational mechanisms, a clearer consensus on goals and priorities, more adequate planning, and prototype developmental, testing, and evaluative efforts.

There are reasons to believe that the gap between readers' needs and the response capabilities of the large research-oriented academic library has been increasing, and is likely to increase even more rapidly in the next decade unless some basic changes can be made in library concepts and capabilities. Furthermore, the prospects for short-term, large reductions in library costs, to be accompanied by large-scale increases in capability, simply through the use of technology as applied to existing library processes, seem relatively dim. In order to achieve significant improvements in the quality or scope of information access or library cost/effectiveness ratios, more basic changes will be required than the "simple" technological replication of many existing library routines and *processes.*

Yet the decade ahead seems likely to be, at best, fiscally austere for both library operations and research and development. The prospects of federal funding are presently bleak, at a time when academic libraries and their parent institutions are likely to be very hard-pressed just in trying to maintain existing quality and major strengths. Thus the dilemma of this report is obvious. Major improvements in library and information access seem clearly possible, at a time when funding for large-scale, complex development and change may be either unavailable or severely limited. If these two assumptions, together with the assumption of a widening gap between needs and response, are true, it still seems essential to proceed. In a period of austerity, the priorities for attack will need to be more carefully chosen; the alternative approaches to be planned, developed, and tested may be reduced; and the time required for perceptible improvements may be longer than might be the case in a period of expanding fiscal support. Nonetheless, if a suitable evolutionary plan of development is devised, it should be possible to go from "here" to "there" at whatever rate of speed the available funds, combined with perceptive planning and development, will permit. It is not altogether unreasonable to anticipate that, in at least some instances, practical demonstrations of significantly improved response capabilities, will elicit further support.

The next several chapters are efforts to describe some of the relevant problems of libraries, to suggest why the gap between response and need may be increasing, and to suggest some specific areas where improved capabilities may be particularly beneficial.

2

SOME CURRENT ASPECTS OF THE LARGE UNIVERSITY LIBRARY[4]

If one is to examine the potentials of technology and other alternatives that might, within reasonable economic and time restraints, improve the cost/effectiveness ratios of the large research library, logic suggests that one should first begin with analyses of (1) the verified long-term needs of users, (2) the library's stated objectives in response to such needs, (3) the degree to which these objectives are presently fulfilled, (4) the relative overall costs attached to each of the major objectives and the priorities that users would attach to these objectives, (5) the cost/effectiveness ratios of suitable alternatives that would "best" fulfill the required objectives, and (6) the trends with respect to past changes and probable future changes in the costs for particular programs or objectives.

While several studies of the use of literature and other kinds of information have been made in a number of libraries and disciplinary areas, there are still large areas which are in urgent need of further investigation. For example, studies are needed in: (1) the determination of effective man-machine interrelationships and requirements, (2) the role of browsing or serendipitous discoveries in using the literature of different subject fields, (3) the present level of users' knowledge and skills in the use of existing bibliographical tools, (4) users' actual requirements in terms of the speed and assurance of access to information or literature, and (5) the optimum specifications for bibliographical or information control systems for different disciplines and groups of users.

At the level of research-oriented use, many readers' stated requirements, when examined critically, are essentially open-ended and, in some instances, opportunistic. In these circumstances libraries have, to some degree, consciously or unconsciously adopted surrogate objectives and, more conspicuously, surrogate measurements of performance. Thus it is not uncommon for a major library objective to be stated in the following manner: "The library will provide access to the information and literature required to meet the cultural, educational, and research functions of the university." Such a statement is translated by faculty and librarians alike into (1) the development of the library's collections within certain limits, often unspecified; (2)

---

[4]Even among libraries of similar size and similar objectives, there are, of course, very significant differences. It is not possible within the scope of this report to deal effectively with these wide variations, or with the similarities or differences that may exist among libraries of substantially different sizes or purposes. By "large university library," I mean the kind of library that falls among the larger academic libraries that share membership in the Association of Research Libraries.

the establishment and maintenance of the necessary bibliographical apparatus; and (3) the provision of the implied services, space, and management. To measure "access," librarians tend to use such factors as the number of journal subscriptions held, the size of the collection, or the number of volumes added during a prior year. These measurements may, in fact, be closely related to potential access, assuming wise selection and internal management, but one cannot assume that potential access, actual use, and needs are identical. The differences obviously become important in the examination of alternatives. It should be emphatically observed that, up to the present time, the alternatives to local, well-organized, systematic collection development, in terms of "access" to scholarly information and literature, have been relatively poor or essentially absent.

In the search for improved cost effectiveness, given the difficulties outlined above, one might simply assume that the broad open-ended objectives of libraries are, in fact, not entirely unreasonable responses to users' needs, and that a reasonable attack on the problem may be made by analyzing the basic purposes for which library expenditures are presently made and then attempting to ascertain how these purposes, services, or products might be provided in superior or less costly ways. The risks here are that the library's present priorities and operations may be partially unresponsive to the current or the long-run requirements of readers, or that the modification of the current operations may inadvertently impair a valuable aspect of user requirements or services. This approach may also be useful in generating desirable data on cost trends.

Although the problems listed above are serious and deserve much more attention than they have had, it is reasonable to suppose that there may also be constructive ways to modify our systems of information and literature access by making certain kinds of stated assumptions. The available evidence on costs, needs, trends, current operations, and related matters, even where the data are not entirely satisfactory, is probably sufficient to support a variety of basic assumptions about the functional utility of present operations and possibly desirable alternatives to them.

Naturally there are risks in connection with such assumptions. A single, rather simple example may be appropriate. Many of the studies and reports on information access and library operations state that the reader needs faster, more assured, and much more convenient access to resources. It is often suggested that the model to be emulated is that of the well-organized, personal library. Clearly this set of objectives must be taken seriously, but the costs may be exponentially related to the degree to which some aspects of the model are attained. Furthermore, individual readers may attach different values to each of these objectives, that is, speed, assurance, and convenience of access. Costs in connection with such variables will also vary sharply from one discipline to another. In choosing objectives, one is quickly and inevitably forced into priority choices in the allocation of limited resources. For example, is the "system" to maximize the absolute size of the resource base, at the price of convenience or speed of access? Or is it to maximize the quality of intellectual analysis and bibliographical control with a consequent reduction in the scope of the resource base? There are clearly many other options.

Since many of the basic objectives or needs of readers are not satisfactorily specified, there is a view that perhaps the design and development of new information- and literature-access systems might best be designed in such a way as to avoid adverse effects on most of the more important existing library capabilities, yet at the same time offer a potential for changing or improving the quality or scope of the services in an incremental and essentially evolutionary manner. With such an approach, one can try to respond to the more visible, immediate needs of libraries and readers; provide for gradual modification or change in emphases; allow for substantial amounts of freedom for individual institutions to respond or modify their operations in an individual manner; and monitor the system in an effort to identify appropriate areas for change or improvement. It is a thesis of this report that the contemporary, large, research-oriented library has become relatively inflexible and can normally respond to new or changing requirements only slowly and often quite inadequately within the limits of available resources.

Thus the balance of this chapter will be devoted to a rather sketchy description of some of the current costs and other trends, pressures, and characteristics of large, scholarly libraries, and the relation of these matters to resource access, to bibliographical control, and to readers' needs or uses. It is assumed that these kinds of factors, taken together, have a direct or inferential bearing on the possible uses of technology. Since there are those who may look to technology as a means of sharply reducing existing library costs, it may be useful to examine absolute library costs, cost trends, relationships to institutional costs, and major categories of expenditure, partly in terms of technological inferences and partly in terms of possible long-term consequences with respect to nontechnological alternatives.

LIBRARY EXPENDITURES, GROWTH TRENDS, AND OTHER CHARACTERISTICS[5]

In 1971-72 aggregate expenditures for 2,500 academic libraries in the United States came to $730 million, excluding capital expenditures for physical plant [12, p. 147]. There were eleven U.S. academic libraries[6] whose

---

[5]It was learned during the drafting of this report that the Council on Library Resources had commissioned Professor W. J. Baumol and his colleagues to undertake a major economic study of academic library costs. This study, *Economics of Academic Libraries* [8], will be published in 1973. The study is much more detailed than the data reported here and should be consulted by anyone seriously interested in library economics.

[6]In rank order with respect to total expenditures: Harvard, Yale, Stanford, University of California at Berkeley, University of California at Los Angeles, University of Michigan, Columbia, Indiana University, University of Illinois, Cornell, University of Minnesota.

expenditures exceeded $5 million in the same year [1]. Among seventy-eight of the larger U.S. and Canadian university libraries belonging to the Association of Research Libraries (ARL), the 1971-72 median level of total expenditures came to $2,855,735; the highest was Harvard, with $9,965,900; the lowest was Saint Louis University, with $1,210,604 [1].

Baumol [7], in a prior study, indicated that library expenditures, for a special aggregate sample of 100 institutions of higher education, have experienced the aggregate rates of increase between 1956 and 1966 shown in table 1.

TABLE 1

Aggregate Amounts and Annual Rates of Change for Designated Library Operations Based on a Sample of 100 Libraries, 1956-66

Aggregate Operation	1956	1966	Approximate Annual Increase (%)
Collection size in volumes	46,990,000	72,050,000	4.4
Enrollment	585,000	1,020,000	5.8
Volumes added per year	1,680,000	4,370,000	10.0
Total operating costs	$27,180,000	$88,260,000	12.5
Salaries and wages	$17,380,000	$50,775,000	10.5
Book expenditures	$6,695,000	$27,860,000	15.0

Source.—[7].
Note.—Unless indicated otherwise, the percentages shown in this and the subsequent tables reflect average, annual, compound percentage growth rates.

Since the institutions in the Baumol sample above are not identical from year to year, data are given in table 2 for fourteen of the larger libraries belonging to the Association of Research Libraries.

With two slightly different institutional samples, some of the trends are examined for categories of library expenditures and operations for a group of "large" and "medium-large" libraries between 1951 and 1970.[7] The fraction of the annual budget of "large" libraries expended for books, periodicals, binding, and other materials has been remarkably constant at about 31

[7]According to the Dunn [21] classification, the "large" university libraries are: California (Berkeley), California (Los Angeles), Chicago, Columbia, Cornell, Harvard, Illinois, Indiana, Michigan, Minnesota, Pennsylvania, Princeton, Stanford, and Yale. The fifteen "medium-large" libraries are: Brown, Duke, Iowa, Johns Hopkins, Louisiana State, Missouri, New York University, North Carolina, Northwestern, Ohio State, Texas, Utah, Virginia, Washington (Seattle), and Wisconsin.

TABLE 2

AGGREGATE AMOUNTS AND ANNUAL RATES OF CHANGE, 1963-71,
FOR DESIGNATED LIBRARY OPERATIONS BASED ON A SAMPLE
OF FOURTEEN LARGE UNIVERSITY LIBRARIES

Aggregate Operation	1963	1971	Approximate Annual Increase (%)
Collection size in volumes	40,866,441	55,113,000	3.8
Volumes added per year	1,570,619	2,209,400	4.4
Annual expenditures for books and binding	$10,679,879	$22,952,000	10.0
Salaries and wages	$21,462,677	$48,965,000	11.0
Total library expenditures	$34,281,609	$78,308,000	11.0

SOURCE.—[1, 1962-63, 1970-71].
NOTE.—The institutions included: California (Berkeley), California (Los Angeles), Chicago, Columbia, Cornell, Duke, Harvard, Illinois, Michigan, Minnesota, Pennsylvania, Princeton, Stanford, Yale. These institutions, with one exception, held the largest collections in 1962-63. The Indiana library was larger than that at Duke, but consistent data for Indiana were not available, so Duke was substituted. By 1970-71, the libraries of Ohio State, Texas, Wisconsin, and Northwestern were larger than those of Pennsylvania, Princeton, and Duke.

percent since 1951. The corresponding figure for the Dunn [21] analysis for "medium-large" libraries has shown an increase to approximately 38 percent, with considerable fluctuation, especially since 1963.

Steeply climbing costs of materials have been nearly matched by a like increase in salaries and wages. Since 1951, expenditures for both have increased at an annual rate of nearly 10 percent. At the same time, staff size and total collection size have increased at an annual rate of 4-5 percent. These data are summarized in table 3.

Unit salaries and wages have been increasing at an average annual rate of 5.1 percent for large libraries and 4.7 percent for medium-large libraries.[8] These figures are similar to the 4.8 percent rate of increase reported by Bowen [11] for professorial salaries.

Unit costs for books and other materials have been increasing at an average annual rate of 3.6 percent for large libraries and 5.3 percent for medium-large libraries.[9] Price indexes for hardcover books, microfilm, periodicals, serial service, and paperback books are given in table 4.

The Consumer Price Index for the period from 1957-59 to 1969 experi-

---

[8]Calculated from the data reported by Dunn [21].
[9]Calculated from the data reported by Dunn [21].

TABLE 3

Average Annual Percentage Increase in Certain Expenditures, Staff, and Collection Size from 1951 to 1970

	Annual Increase (%)	
	"Large" Libraries	"Medium-large" Libraries
Expenditures for salaries and wages	9.7	10.0
Total staff size	4.4	5.1
Expenditures for acquisitions	10.2	11.7
Volumes in collection	3.6	4.8

Source.—Calculated from data in [21].

enced an average annual increase of 2.2 percent. It is instructive to compare this figure to those in table 4. Except for microfilm, library materials are increasing in price far out of proportion to other consumer commodities, and recent rates of increase are believed to be substantially higher than those shown. This is especially true for serial subscription costs.

Other summary data and trends are presented in the following references [1, 7, 8, 20, 27, 57].

LIBRARY EXPENDITURES—RELATIONSHIP TO INSTITUTIONAL TRENDS

To the extent that these data are reliable,[10] the average large and medium-large research library, contrary to some impressions, does not seem to be taking an ever larger percentage of its parent institution's current expenditures. Furthermore, the average library's percentage of total institutional expenditures for educational and general purposes seems to be relatively small. In his analysis of academic library cost trends for the National Advisory Commission on Libraries, Baumol and his associates [7] point out that average library expenditures as a percentage of institutional total expenditures for general and educational purposes rose from 3.0 percent in 1959–60 to 3.3 percent in 1963–64, where they remained through 1965–66 (estimated). The averages are based on data for some 1,951 (1959–60) to 2,207 (1966) colleges and universities.

In order to examine the relationship between institutional and library expenditures for a group of larger libraries, data were gathered for twenty-

[10]There are serious questions about the consistency, comparability, and many other aspects of most of the existing library and institutional cost data.

CHAPTER 2

TABLE 4

PRICE INDEXES FOR LIBRARY BOOKS AND OTHER MATERIALS

Commodity	Base Period	To Date	Index	Average Annual Increase (%)
Hardcover books	1957-59	1969	177.1	5.3
Paperback books	1962	1969	171.7	8.0
Periodicals	1957-59	1970	211.6	6.4
Serial services.......	1957-59	1970	214.7	6.6
Microfilm	1959	1969	118.6	1.7

SOURCE.—"Prices of U.S. and Foreign Published Materials," in [12, 1970, 1971].

four of the twenty-nine "large" and "medium-large" universities as they were defined in the Dunn study [21]. Library expenditures as a percentage of general and educational expenditures were calculated for each of the libraries for the years 1945-46, 1950-51, 1955-56, 1960-61, 1965-66, 1967-68, and 1969-70. The results are presented in table 5.

It will be noted that the mean percentage of educational and general expenditures for the medium-large to large university library has declined from 1950-51. For the past fifteen years it has remained constant at about 3.7 percent. The maximum-minimum range for this percentage has also narrowed. A closer analysis indicates that the largest libraries tend to be at the lower percentage levels, while the smaller libraries within the group tend to be above the median. There are exceptions.

These percentages of institutional general and educational expenditures for library purposes are also in substantial agreement with the data cited by Dix [19, p. 24] for various groups of institutions for the period 1930-50. For example, Dix, citing Millet [38, p. 107], gives library expenditures, as a percentage of educational expense, as 2.8 percent in 1930, 3.8 percent in 1940, and 3.4 percent in 1950.

It is recognized that the general and educational expenditures of a university will include research grants, fellowship support, and other expenditures that may seem to have little effect upon the needs for library services. In fact, some programs funded in this manner quite often make extraordinarily large demands upon the library and its resources, without commensurate funding or support. The growth of restricted funding may result in library expenditures requiring a larger and larger percentage of the average institution's unrestricted funds; data are not available to clarify this question.

LIBRARY EXPENDITURES—PER CAPITA STUDENT BASIS

The relationship between library expenditures and institutional expendi-

TABLE 5

LIBRARY EXPENDITURES AS A PERCENTAGE OF GENERAL
AND EDUCATIONAL EXPENDITURES FOR TWENTY-FOUR
"LARGE" AND "MEDIUM-LARGE" UNIVERSITIES
FROM 1945 TO 1970

Year	Maximum	Minimum	Median	Mean
1945-46	8.0	1.3	3.9	4.1
1950-51	8.3	1.3	3.55	4.2
1955-56	6.9	1.7	3.7	3.8
1960-61	7.6	1.4	3.2	3.7
1965-66	6.3	1.6	3.75	3.7
1967-68	6.7	1.6	3.45	3.7
1969-70	6.9	2.1	3.35	3.7

SOURCE.—University general and educational expenditures were obtained from the institutions themselves, in response to a brief questionnaire. It was possible to include the nonresponding land-grant universities in the sample by referring to [57]. Library expenditures were obtained from [1, 1944-45 to 1969-70]. All data for 1967-68 are from [20]. The data for 1969-70 are from [27].

NOTE.—The institutions included are: Brown, California (Berkeley), Chicago, Columbia, Cornell, Duke, Harvard, Illinois, Indiana, Iowa, Louisiana State, Minnesota, Missouri, New York University, North Carolina, Northwestern, Ohio State, Pennsylvania, Stanford, Texas, University of Washington, Virginia, Wisconsin, Yale.

tures may also be examined on a cost-per-student basis. In the Baumol study [7], college and university library expenditures per student were shown to have increased at an annual rate of 5.1 percent between 1951 and 1966.

Bowen has indicated that there has been an annual average increase of 7.5-8.1 percent in the total cost per student in a small sample of private universities between 1905 and 1966 [11, pp. 19-21]. These two figures are, of course, based upon entirely different institutional samples, and hence may differ for that reason alone. Because of sharp variations among institutions in the ratios of undergraduate to graduate enrollment, in the sizes of student bodies, in the degree of faculty involvement in research, and in the relative importance given to historical, literary, and other disciplinary areas that make heavy library demands as against those that do not have such extensive library requirements, it is likely that per-student library costs will vary quite sharply from one institution to another.

LIBRARY EXPENDITURES—PHYSICAL PLANT

The regularly available data for academic institutions and libraries normally include neither physical plant maintenance costs nor the capital costs for physical plant. It is possible to estimate incremental library physical plant costs very roughly. Among the academic members of the Association of Research Libraries the median net number of volumes added in 1971-72 was reported at 81,273. This would represent an annual growth rate of 5.5 percent if it were based on the 1,486,412 volume holdings of the median library in terms of collection size [1]. If we assume book stack capacity at 15 volumes per square foot, there will be an initial, annual, incremental space requirement of some 5,420 net usable square feet, with subsequent annual requirements increasing exponentially in proportion to the net growth of the collections.

The larger university libraries are growing at a slower rate but, of course, occupy more space. In the sample of larger university libraries (see table 2), the average, annual, compounded collection growth rate from 1963 to 1971 was 3.8 percent. This growth rate, unless it declines further (e.g., Harvard added at the rate of 2.5 percent in 1970-71), points to the doubling of book space requirements in eighteen to nineteen years. The median collection size among these larger libraries, as shown in table 2, is 3,600,000 volumes, and the average growth rate would result in an initial annual increase of 135,000 volumes.[11] At 15 volumes per net square foot, the initial annual space requirement would come to 9,000 net square feet.

If it is arbitrarily assumed that the construction cost of such space was thirty dollars per net usable square foot, the median ARL library would require $162,600 in the first incremental year, and a slowly increasing amount thereafter in proportion to the annual increase in acquisitions and construction costs. The comparable amount for the large university library would come to $270,000. To these totals, annual space maintenance costs of, say, one dollar per square foot should be added, bringing the first-year totals to $168,020 and $279,000 for the median and large university library.

Based upon median total library expenditures in 1970-71 of $2,776,105 for the ARL median library and $5,802,000 for the median expenditure level of the large library group in table 2, the initial-year physical space costs might, in effect, add approximately 6.1 and 4.8 percent, respectively, to the annual budgets of these libraries.

Of course, universities do not budget space maintenance costs or capital expenditures in this manner. Nonetheless, these or related amounts must be recognized as a part of the costs of having and operating a library.

EXPENDITURES, GROWTH, AND OTHER LIBRARY CHARACTERISTICS
There is a very rapid escalation in the cost of library material and

---

[11]The calculation above is very conservative. The actual median for gross additions in 1970-71 would have fallen between Cornell and Stanford, if based upon gross size of collections. Cornell added 175,232 volumes and Stanford added 173,721 volumes.

labor—just "to stay even." The recent rates of increase almost certainly exceed institutional long-term resources that can be made available for library support [11, p. 54]. It should be noted that six of the eleven largest university libraries are in privately supported universities. These institutions may be in greater fiscal jeopardy than are some tax-supported universities, but recent studies by the Carnegie Commission on Higher Education indicate that fiscal difficulties may be the rule rather than the exception in both publicly and privately supported institutions.

The current output of literature and information is rising at a higher rate than libraries individually can absorb, and the increase is not being absorbed collectively under existing patterns of acquisition. A portion of this increase is reflected in increases variously estimated at 3-6 percent annual (i.e., births less deaths) growth in the number of new serial titles, to which there must be added serial price increases in many fields rising at 10-15 percent annually. The devaluation of the dollar may have a more serious impact upon the library than it has on any other part of the university.

In response to the growth of knowledge there may be an increasing tendency for scholarly specialization that has the effect of narrowing the scope of individual research investigations for some scholars. This trend, if it exists, does not necessarily narrow the library's acquisition responsibilities. These responsibilities are a direct reflection of the full range of academic programs and fields of research. Since World War II, there has been a substantial expansion in the number of teaching and research fields in the majority of universities. Such expansions, for example, have been conspicuous in the foreign area programs which have often imposed upon libraries costly acquisition and processing burdens for materials in esoteric languages, without commensurate funding.

There has been a substantial increase in the number of graduate students and faculty members in many universities. The expectations of these persons as to information or literature access have tended to increase both quantitatively and qualitatively. The slight use cited in [16] is not universal.

A number of the major studies of the informational needs of investigators in the physical, biological, and social sciences have asserted that there are serious requirements for improved access to the literature of the disciplines, to large machine-readable factual data banks, and to new bibliographical tools or literature control mechanisms. There have been a number of statements of scholarly anxiety that the volume of literature has grown so large, or is growing so large, that greatly improved bibliographical and intellectual control devices are needed to establish the degree of quality and the degree of relevance of various kinds of material relating to any given problem or topic. A few have suggested that we need systems to suppress, lose, or destroy "worthless" or redundant information as well as to synthesize that which has substantive value. There are also observers who point out that serendipitous discoveries in the literature are commonplace and that existing systems may be deficient in matching stated interests with relevant literature or data. It is clear that much more needs to be learned about users' informational requirements, the ways in which these can best be fulfilled, and readers' interaction with existing and alternative modes of access.

Despite rapid increases in expenditures, the typical research library is visibly hard pressed, and is not presently in a strong position to respond, either qualitatively or quantitatively, to additional burdens or new demands. It has typically had little or no money for the internal analysis of its own operations, and even less for the experimental development and testing of alternative solutions.

The library is critically dependent for most of its operations and services upon extremely large and (in many cases) extremely complex files. The largest of these files is typically the dictionary card catalog of a library's holdings which may, for a reasonably large university library, contain from 3 to 8 million cards with new cards being added at the rate of several thousand a week. Each card may contain several hundred characters, including characters in almost all the languages and alphabets of the world. There are, in addition, many other files: for example, shelf lists; departmental catalogs and shelf lists; a variety of status or processing files, including outstanding orders, in-bindery, circulation, and borrower files; serial holdings files; etc.

To build and maintain these files requires a substantial part of the total staff budget. Not all users know how to use them well. Filing rules may be extremely complex, and even the sophisticated user may be unable to find wanted materials. Some of the files are so large and complex as to inhibit, quite seriously, changes in cataloging concepts, the updating and subdividing of old subject headings, or even the permanent relocation of a book. Many of the files are maintained and used in highly formal ways for purposes of action or decision making.

It has been noted that the library is a labor-intensive enterprise. A very high proportion of its labor costs are related primarily to data-base maintenance and use relating to the procurement, processing, and provision of access to recorded information.

At the present time much of the more costly and complex data contained in the typical, large university library catalog appears to be relatively little used. A careful study of the use of the main public catalog in the Yale University Library revealed that 73 percent of the users of the catalog were attempting a search for a particular, known document; 16 percent were attempting a subject search; 6 percent were attempting to find what works were held by the library from a known author or other source; and 5 percent were attempting a bibliographic search without intending to use the identified documents.

It was concluded that only 56 percent of the searches were for a document as an end in itself; the objective of the balance of searches was for subject information rather than a specific document [34, 35]. Community two-year colleges and other institutions may, of course, have very different patterns of card catalog use. Other studies have shown that many of the functions of reference retrieval and "current awareness" by scholars are fulfilled by relatively informal information access channels. These data suggest the importance of examining more carefully and critically the functions and alternatives that should be considered in modifying library catalogs and other bibliographic tools.

A significant percentage of the books in a large research collection are very infrequently used; for example, the average frequency of use per title may, for substantial parts of a large research collection, be as low as one use in fifty years or more. With varying degrees of difficulty the titles with the lowest probability of use can be predicted. The frequencies of use vary sharply according to subject field [24]. It must be emphasized that if high frequency of use is taken as the *sole* criterion for building a research collection, much of the material in the social sciences, most of that in the humanities, virtually all historical sources, and all older materials in the biological and physical sciences would be excluded. For this reason frequency of use must be examined very critically as only one of many factors in considering alternative systems of resource access, but it surely is relevant to the design of any alternative system of access that might provide several different levels of accessibility to research-related materials.

It is evident that there are serious geographic and institutional imbalances in the extent of the research resources available in the country. There are some compelling reasons for trying to develop economically viable systems that might reduce these imbalances. The leading universities, with the largest libraries, are somewhat ambivalent about any measures that might seem to reduce their relative institutional position in terms of resource strength. There are also anxieties related to casual assumptions that these libraries can readily fulfill the needs of much larger constituencies.

One must recognize that most of the modern books and journals that are now in the typical university or college library are printed on paper that will disintegrate in the foreseeable future unless remedial action to treat the paper is taken. The disintegration of the paper is primarily the result of acidic substances in the paper itself or in the size with which the paper was coated in manufacture. A simple, large-scale, tested, and inexpensive method for neutralizing the acid content is not presently available, though some promising research has been done and such a capability may be announced soon.

The corpus of the literature and information pertinent to research may seem to be so large and growing so rapidly as to be essentially unmanageable. If the corpus is divided into suitable segments by form, period, country of origin, language, and subject, it may present a more manageable set of problems. For example, there are some current estimates that perhaps the number of current serials on a worldwide basis (excluding house organs, newspapers, government documents, and a few other categories) may be around 100,000–175,000 titles with a net annual growth of perhaps as "little" as 3 or 4 percent. Since some large research libraries are now said to be receiving as many as 50,000 serial titles, the gap between existing holdings and the total corpus may not be as large as one might expect.

CONCLUSION

A few observers have stated that the scholarly library is in—or is rapidly approaching—a state of crisis. There are some who disagree. The existing or impending crisis may be more severe for the large research-oriented library than it is for the college or smaller university library. The library profession and the scholars who are served by libraries have clearly recognized many of the key elements in the circumstances leading to real or potential crises. However, the required organizational, planning, fiscal, research, and developmental mechanisms to generate adequate responses are absent or relatively weak. There may be some professional and scholarly ambivalence, and possibly even some lack of logic, in examining the actions that could or should be taken to modify and improve the overall cost effectiveness of the existing research library and the related information systems and processes. There are many experts, each with a different "solution." There is some tendency to postpone serious modifications in the present library "system" on the assumption that all the problems will be solved by an "external" technology. There are technologists who have asserted that computers with very high-density storage capacities at very low cost; with low-cost, wide-band circuitry reaching every home and office; with very low-cost, very high-density microforms; and with other devices—some probable, some unlikely—will "solve" the "problem."

Licklider, in writing on networks [9, pp. 310–11], clearly indicated some of the current difficulties:

> One of the difficulties of network planning at the present time stems from the fact that while "realistic" planning is limited by external factors to a time span of five or ten years, computer-based information networks will be developing and evolving for two or three times five or ten years. Networks planned now can be no more than way stations and checkpoints on a long road. But the road itself and where it goes are of the very greatest importance for the future of mankind. It may well be that networks planned now will be significant more because of their influence on the laying out and building of the road than because of their improvement of library and information services. It is easier to see and describe the information networks of two or three decades hence, I think, than the course that network efforts will follow in the decade now beginning.

It is increasingly evident, as one examines the issues, that there are at least five interrelated sets of problems: (1) the adequacy of the organizational and conceptual mechanisms for effecting desired changes in the systems of information and literature access, (2) the current state and prospective rates of change in the relevant technologies and other alternatives, (3) the functional objectives to be sought, (4) the desired or feasible rates of change or evolution, and (5) the funds available for development and ongoing support of the system.

A relatively strong case can be made for the following generalizations: (1) An evolutionary pattern of library change is necessary, feasible, and desirable. (2) These changes should be more extensive and more basic than many of the present efforts would suggest. (3) Many initial requirements have been or can be satisfactorily specified—although there is a need to know much more about requirements. (4) User, as well as institutional, habits and attitudes will need to change in some respects. (5) Much of the necessary funding may have to be provided by changing some library concepts and objectives. (6) There are, among the desirable, necessary, and feasible changes, a number that are essentially nontechnological, or that may use technology in combination with nontechnological developments.

To achieve important changes in costs or in the scope of library services or resources, at least three kinds of change will be required: (1) some basic changes in current library processes and functions; (2) the development of relatively large-scale, highly effective, interdependent systems of literature, data, and bibliographical access; and (3) substantial but cost/effective use of fairly sophisticated technologies—collectively developed or used.

Changes in the following areas may be particularly beneficial—or even imperative—in the next several years: (1) changes in the concepts of the bibliographical apparatus for scholarship, with a "decoupling" of much of the bibliographical apparatus from the holdings of any single institution; (2) an effort to start, and to extend as rapidly as possible, the use in citations of International Standard Book Numbers (ISBN) and International Standard Serial Numbers (ISSN) to assist in the location of wanted materials; (3) the development of one or more effective joint resource-access mechanisms for current serial and other publications; and (4) the extended use of computers in handling bibliographic and library operational data.

Extensive use of microforms may have important relationships to resource access, especially for retrospective materials, but the potential is presently difficult to estimate. Computer output microform (COM) may be extremely important in the field of bibliography. Substantial increases in fast-access, low-cost computer storage; the availability of low-cost, wide-band communications capability; new photographic and other techniques for high-density data storage; and any major trend for the utilization of linked audiovisual and computer technologies in the independent learning or instructional processes in institutions of higher education, could each be expected to have an impact on the library. The exact probabilities and effects are difficult to predict. Further attention to most of these matters is given in Chapters 3, 4, 5, and 6.

3

BIBLIOGRAPHICAL AND LIBRARY PROCESSING FUNCTIONS

There are some compelling reasons to examine, with a relatively high priority, library "processing" operations, including cataloging and many other functions, in terms of long-term alternatives for bibliographical access and control, potential changes in library concepts or operations, and technological potentials. Library processing costs may consume approximately 30 percent of total library expenditures and equal the expenditures for books, journals, and other materials.[12] The processing functions of a library are largely file-oriented, involving quite complex files and data. The decision-making functions in many aspects of processing are highly formal in nature. These are two characteristics that theoretically match computer capabilities. Furthermore, the speed, accuracy, and quality of many library processing functions are critical to the library's basic responsiveness to user needs and other performance characteristics. A major end product of a large portion of processing operations is the public and ancillary card catalogs; yet the card catalog, especially in the larger scholarly libraries, may not be serving many readers' needs very effectively [34, 52]. Such catalogs have, in any case, become so large and unwieldy as to make them virtually unadaptable to changing subject concepts and changes in terminology as well as inflexible in terms of simplication or other revisions in cataloging or filing rules. In consequence, at some time in the reasonably near future a number of research libraries may conclude that the existing card catalog will best be "closed" for materials as of a given imprint date, and a new alternative, or alternatives, created. The Library of Congress is giving such consideration to its own catalogs.

Many library processing functions are highly "customized," or locally oriented in ways that may create few benefits except a degree of compatibility with older, local subject headings, forms of entry, and other variants from more or less "standard procedures." There was a period in which most of the intellectual input into library processing systems and catalogs was generated locally. This is no longer the case. A very significant portion of the data now required for the selection, acquisition, and cataloging of current publications is generated in standard formats, much of it machine-readable, by institutions and agencies that are external to the academic library.

These various observations point to some fairly central issues. How can we

---

[12]Satisfactory data on this point do not appear to be available. For general observations on the matter by Rutherford Rogers and others, see [45, pp. 83-85].

best avoid either processing functions or the building of expensive tools that may not be effective? How can we best exploit existing technologies and available data to create more effective literature and informational access? How could we accomplish these objectives at lower costs than now prevail?

Much of the contemporary literature having to do with bibliographical access, as it relates to libraries, and especially as it deals with card catalogs, seems to pose some relatively simple choices in terms of technological change or development, for example: (1) to use the computer essentially to generate catalog cards or to print, in book form, tools that are essentially card catalogs in terms of content, or (2) to use the computer as a means of file access in an interactive, search and display capacity, utilizing, it is assumed, either an institutional bibliographic data base, a regional one such as that developing for the Ohio College Library Center, or a series of separate, but overlapping, disciplinary bases such as that for MEDLARS in the field of medicine.

It is evident in this situation that there are many critical variables as to what may constitute an appropriate bibliographical data base; how the data base may be affected by the needs of different groups of users or by the needs of different library functions; the kinds of access to, or outputs from, any given data base that are likely to be most useful to readers, to libraries; etc.

A highly schematic outline of a few of the historical changes in the evolution of scholarly libraries and their bibliographical tools may be suggestive. The earliest libraries established their social or intellectual domain, as it were, through the textual resources that were collected and made available to readers. At a later point, some of these libraries started to build simple bibliographical tools that would aid or even supplant the human curator in terms of knowledge about the library's holdings and the location of the holdings within the library. As serial publications came along, one saw the gradual emergence of indexing or abstracting tools to control the content of serial publications. These were prepared and distributed independently of the serial publications themselves and independently of the content or holdings of any single library. With only a few exceptions scholarly libraries show in their catalogs only serial *titles*. The information is needed in order to locate a desired title within a library. There may be in some instances subject references to serial titles, but this process, for obvious reasons, lacks great precision or reliability as a guide to pertinent materials or the contents of cited serials. Many libraries have, in addition, published local lists of serials, giving the library's call numbers or locations. There are also many union lists of serial publications that indicate the institutions holding a given serial title, though the actual call numbers or locations of the titles within a given institution are seldom indicated.

As one compares the systems for controlling serials with those for monographs, it is evident that there is still a major local development of an elaborate bibliographical apparatus, primarily the card catalog and related tools, that attempts to provide subject, title, and author access to those monographs held by the local library. The card catalog, unlike the usual published abstracting or indexing tools for serials, thus fulfills both locational and bibliographical functions. The major development in recent years of externally generated bibliographical data for monographic materials has been thought of primarily as a means of reducing the labor costs associated with the maintenance of local cataloging processes. It would appear that 50-90 percent of the basic intellectual cataloging data for *current* monographs, depending largely upon language, may now be available to many scholarly libraries from external sources, for example, from the *National Union Catalog*, MARC II data, and other sources. These data have become extremely important in reducing the costs of maintaining local bibliographical tools, primarily the card catalog. The data are also used for selection, preparing purchase orders, and other important functions.

However, a more basic or significant use of these data on monographs may be for the creation of a very wide variety of printed, general and specialized indices. These would be updated frequently according to the velocity of change and output in the monographic literature. Such indices could be reformatted, restructured, and cumulated as a discipline or segment of literature changes and grows. The tools could be designed to appeal both to institutions and to individuals as subscribers. The technologies to be used would, of course, be the machine-readable bibliographical data base and computer photocomposition, which has radically altered the economic feasibility of catalog formatting, updating, and printing. If such bibliographical tools were to be generated nationally, the market could be a large one, and the unit costs might be relatively modest.

One can easily see that specialized, printed bibliographies could also be generated locally, based upon local or regional as well as national holdings. The costs would be higher. These devices would not initially displace the card catalog for retrospective imprints, and might not supplant a simpler inventory card catalog for all imprints held by a library. Nor would such bibliographies, whether nationally or locally oriented, displace batch or interactive searches of suitable, bibliographical machine-readable data bases when there were requirements that made such searches necessary or more appropriate than a specialized, printed bibliographical tool or index.

In summary, it is evident that there may now be a technology to create a versatile set of bibliographies of monographic as well as serial literature, tailored to a wide spectrum of user needs, that need not be based, in terms of scope or content, upon the holdings of any single library. Such bibliographies might improve reader access to recorded literature,[13] be more convenient to

---

[13]There are indications that many scholarly readers may not be very systematic in their pursuit of pertinent literature in terms of using either library catalogs or existing bibliographies. See, e.g. [33, pp. 87-88].

use, and greatly simplify and reduce local processing costs. If handled nationally, these tools might have many of the capabilities of some current selective dissemination of information (SDI) systems in which users' interest profiles are matched, by computer, with machine-readable bibliographies—at relatively high cost. Such tools could mitigate some of the problems of uneven geographic and institutional resource access. Obviously there are many unstated problems with the developments proposed, but some alternative to the growing restraints of the card catalog seems essential. The interactive machine search of a large data base, reflecting local, regional, or national holdings, may be a partial response, but the economics seem likely to be poor for very large files except in special instances. Many institutions or individuals may be unable for some time to afford such access, and there are few data as yet to suggest that readers will universally find the console-based search an efficient mechanism for *all* purposes. In fact, much more critical scrutiny of the user's relationship to, and effective use of, the entire bibliographical control or access "system" seems relatively urgent. The major points to be emphasized here are that there can now be a broad range of choices, based upon the utilization of some important major variables: (1) the scope and nature of the most appropriate data bases for given sets of requirements, and (2) the modes of access to and utilization of such data bases. Simply printing catalog cards, for local holdings, from a MARC II data base, with the cards to be filed into a conventional multimillion card catalog, does not reflect, from the user's viewpoint, any basic functional improvement in literature access—or a very significant, long-term use of technology.

It will be noted at once that most of the existing serial or other generalized bibliographies or a simple footnote citation require the reader to search in a local bibliographic tool—usually the card catalog or a list of serial titles—to ascertain whether the library holds the desired item, and if so, where it is located within the library. It is evident that much of the existing use of the card catalog is solely for this purpose in some institutions [34]. Having found the item and its location, the user may not find the desired material on the shelf, and a further search may be required. These routines require a very substantial amount of reader time and energy. It is therefore important to ask whether there may not be some mechanisms that could reduce this burden. Obviously a computer search of a bibliographical data base either could be coupled automatically to a request for designated documents or could be mediated by a human operator, as in the Ohio State University Library's on-line circulation system. There may be other helpful alternatives.

If one were to extend the use of the International Standard Book Numbers and the International Standard Serial Numbers into the bibliographical apparatus in all of its aspects as quickly as possible, these data could be used very advantageously to reduce and simplify the processes of determining whether a given library has a cited item, where it is located in that library, and whether it is available. Such control numbers could also simplify and hasten many internal library operations. If such numbers could be made a commonplace part of all major bibliographical tools and citations, a reader who needed materials carrying such numbers could almost completely bypass the current expenditure of effort in trying to ascertain the "correct" catalog entry and the subsequent processes of determining whether the local library has a wanted item and, if so, where it is located and its availability status. This would be accomplished by building such numbers into a library's bibliographical system in such a way that the standard numbers would lead directly or indirectly to the locally held item. Libraries could, in fact, at very low costs, generate holdings catalogs by such numbers only. Thus the burden of checking whether the library had a given title (whose standard number was known) could entirely bypass the conventional card catalog. A relatively simple computer-based file could also be used by means of the telephone, through which the wanted book number could be dialed, with an oral, prerecorded message on status, and, if the item were available, the means of handling a request by a reader-identification number. The book could subsequently be delivered by messenger or otherwise made available. Such a universal numbering system clearly could also be a powerful device in simplifying interinstitutional access to resources and building simple union catalogs, and could assist in the capture for local purposes of machine-readable bibliographical data.[14]

This proposal is rather seriously oversimplified. The International Standard Book Numbers will appear, at best, only in currently published materials, and it will take some time for a sufficient body of materials with numbers to accumulate to be useful.[15] More seriously, there is no "bibliographical linkage" in the numbers between various editions, reprints, or even variant bindings of given works. Thus a reader might request a cited ISBN item, but should the local library hold only an earlier or a later edition, the response would be negative. It is possible, but not simple, to build a machine-based system of linkages. However, in the case of many scholarly titles there is likely to be only a single edition, and for these the approach could be simple and potentially extremely useful. There are other critical problems. Even so, it seems that (1) some significant means must be found to reduce the present effort required of the reader to secure locally held materials, (2) a partial separation of much of the basic bibliographical apparatus from the holdings of the single institution may be a step in the direction of improved

---

[14]There is presently a Louisiana Numerical Register Union Catalog, with 650,000 entries based upon Library of Congress catalog card numbers. The international standard numbers could eventually prove more powerful if widely cited and given in publications. LC catalog numbers may appear in an increasing percentage of domestic publications; it is not reasonable to expect them to be shown in foreign publications or bibliographical references.

[15]It has been estimated that between 80 and 85 percent of current, i.e., 1973, U.S. trade publications are carrying ISBNs—not always accurately or completely.

access and economy for many purposes, and (3) the widespread coupling of bibliographical tools and citations with international standard numbers might help to simplify long-term access processes for both users and libraries. A shift to the design and publication of a wide variety of expendable, printed, bibliographical tools—on a national basis—may provide a faster, more inclusive, and very much more dynamic and responsive system of bibliographical control and access than is presently available. Because of the scale of operations, such bibliographical tools might make efficient instead of what otherwise may be relatively inefficient use of some important technologies. Furthermore, the development of such tools would basically enhance the potential uses of computer-stored bibliographic data by means of terminals in an on-line, interactive mode where such uses offered greater cost/effectiveness ratios.

It is clear, if one were persuaded that this sort of bibliographical development were desirable, that scholarly institutions and libraries at the present time lack the required organizational structure to plan and develop such a system. It is assumed that this is not an insuperable obstacle if the goals otherwise seem desirable.

Almost all aspects of library data processing and other file-related functions are suitable candidates for computer data processing. The obstacles are those of effective systems design, the determination of suitable objectives, and funding. The cost effectiveness of new systems in relation to present systems cannot be ignored. It is certainly feasible at present to design and build bibliographical (and literature) access systems that are superior to those now available; but there must also be assurance that such systems can be funded. Further discussions of these matters are presented in Chapter 5.

With the passage of time, it is evident that many scholarly informational needs are not limited to literature and citations or references. There are needs for specific factual data—including that available only in machine-readable form. The pressures for such access will surely increase. There are many obvious problems relating to the privacy of such data, the manner of data collection and organization, the quality or validity of the data, etc. It has been argued that the provision of access to such data files is a research library obligation. The library, in fact, would appear to be the most logical institution to provide such access. However, within the limitations of the present computer and communications technologies, it would seem that the actual data bases and search capabilities could be located in a few regional or national centers, with each center responsible for a broad spectrum of subjects, and offering either remote, off-line query capabilities and batch searching or on-line query and search, depending upon the size and nature of the data base, the load on the system, the structure of the search, the distance, the needs of the user, and the terminal systems available.

Exactly the same pattern of organization may be appropriate for computer-based searches of the major, general and discipline- or mission-oriented bibliographical data bases for readers and libraries. The continuous use of such bibliographical data bases by a library for its own operations including selection, acquisition, and other functions may also justify machine data-base maintenance and access. However, the question of how access to very large files can be most advantageously provided should be resolved by careful economic, technical, and functional analyses rather than by some a priori design specification. It would appear highly unlikely that either load requirements or the costs of such access would justify widespread local file maintenance and search capability of major discipline-oriented literature data bases for some time. These patterns of access may require user charges under some circumstances as well as regional or national access systems.

A number of studies of the current state of information and literature access in various disciplinary fields point to an urgent need to improve the systems for the qualitative evaluation of literature and the establishment of more precise measures of relevance among literature, information, and user needs. These are issues that the library has, for the most part, avoided. More basic solutions to the relevance and quality problems are clearly dependent upon further long-term analyses, but the problems may be reduced by the emergence of a spectrum of bibliographical tools meeting a variety of different criteria for coverage or inclusion. The quality, scope, and accessibility of a bibliographical system may ultimately influence constructively the systems related to document or literature acquisition and distribution.

The suggestions outlined here may imply that the present structure of the bibliographical apparatus for scholarship is a simple one. Such an impression would be false, for the structure is extraordinarily complex. The "system" is highly segmented and pluralistic; there are insufficient standards; there are redundant services; there are serious gaps in coverage; and there are serious concerns about the intellectual adequacy of the system. These are not, however, persuasive arguments for the indefinite postponement of an evolutionary pattern of change and rationalization of bibliographical functions and access [28]. Potentials for change in bibliographical systems are very critically related to technology, and, within technology, to computers and to COM (computer output microform) and other means of storing, manipulating, and displaying or distributing bibliographical data. Some aspects of these matters are dealt with in the succeeding chapters.[16]

---

[16]An important review by Basil Stuart-Stubbs [49] on alternatives to the card catalog, problems of union catalogs, the use of ISBN numbers, and the use of COM in connection with catalogs, reached us after the basic draft of this report had been completed. Mr. Stuart-Stubbs and I independently reached somewhat similar conclusions.

4

SHARED RESOURCES, PHOTOCOPYING, AND FACSIMILE TRANSMISSION

SHARED RESOURCES

The library literature for some years has acknowledged that no library can be autonomous in meeting a broad spectrum of research needs, and that the sharing of resources is necessary. There is some ambivalence, however, about the concepts of sharing that tends not to be stated clearly. Many scholars and other users are probably distrustful of any plan that locates in a remote institution any significant portion of the resources required, or potentially required, by an investigator or student. It is already difficult enough to secure materials in many instances from one's local library. Thus, while resource autonomy for the single institution is recognized as unattainable, there seem to have been tacit assumptions that the present pattern of aggregate acquisitions among institutions, perhaps with a little more structuring and some improvement in the institutional mechanisms for sharing, will meet the gap between the relevant, aggregate output of printed and other research materials and the holdings of any one institution.

Clearly this is a complex problem. It is, in part, a reflection of what is described by some as information overload or the "information explosion." It is, in part, a reflection of a substantially broader spectrum of academic interests and research. It is, in part, a set of issues that relate to the ways in which pertinent literature or information in the broadest sense are covered and used. There are those who would prefer to cut off a portion of the redundant or insignificant growth at its source; those who do not regard the problems as serious; those who regard the document itself as obsolete; and those who say that technology will take care of the problem through ultra-microforms, microwave channels, holography, or some other innovative measure. In many of these proposals the technological relief is to become available at some reasonably distant time in the future. Some have assumed that bibliographical or information searching and textual access can be directly coupled. It is clear that, in fact, some of these things *can* be done, at least up to a point. The questions are what systems of resource development and access are likely to be optimal in terms of overall costs and effectiveness for scholarly work. Current efforts to improve the systems of access need not impede or interfere with future technological or other innovative solutions to these problems; they may, in fact, encourage or stimulate such developments.

Collection growth rates in most of the major university libraries at the present time range between 3 and 6 percent compounded annually. These growth rates may not sound ominous, but they represent substantial investments in materials, space, and processing costs. At the end of fiscal 1971-72 there were sixty-seven U.S. and Canadian university libraries with 1 million or more volumes. Twenty-one of these had 2 million or more volumes, and thirteen reported in excess of 3 million [1]. Since there are more than 2,500 institutions of higher education, it is evident that the multimillion volume collections are located in a conspicuous numerical minority of institutions. However, it is in this minority of institutions that most of the advanced research takes place, and it is argued that even these institutions are unable to keep up with the estimated 5-15 percent annual rates of growth in the current literature output[17]—let alone fill in retrospective gaps in their collections.

The objectives in connection with the sharing of resources are presumably (1) to improve the quality or to extend the absolute body of resources available; (2) in some manner to improve the scope, quality, or assurance of access for many users; and (3) to improve the present cost/effectiveness ratios as they relate to both aggregate and local resource availability.

There seem to be relatively few ways through which resources may be shared without going to rather novel (and thus far rather expensive) technological solutions: (1) There is the existing pattern of essentially informal, decentralized institutional sharing through interlibrary loan. (2) There are more formally structured, but still decentralized, institutional sharing patterns in the manner of the Association of Research Libraries' Farmington Plan for foreign acquisitions,[18] in some state contractual systems, or in a more recent proposal for designating specific institutions as "national or regional centers of excellence" with federal funding to support the costs of external or interstate use and, if possible, to assist in supporting collection development in the designated subject fields. (3) There have also been proposals for federally supported regional or national acquisition and loan centers that would not be directly associated with, or operated by, an existing university or research library. (4) There are a number of instances in which two or more institutions in close geographic proximity agree, informally or formally, to share resources, for example, Duke and North Carolina or the Joint Universities Library at Vanderbilt. (5) There are formally shared and supported central pools of commonly owned and used resources, with the two most notable examples being the Center for Research Libraries in Chicago and the National Lending Library for Science and Technology in Boston Spa, England. In a variant of the "pool" concept, the possibility has been suggested of using large-scale micro-reproduction of materials to which an institution might have access by the distribution of copies, by loan from the

---

[17]For example, Anderla of the University of Paris has predicted an annual output by 1985 of 12-14 million unduplicated "items" of scientific and technical information as compared with about 2 million such items at present [2].

[18]This plan was from the beginning essentially an acquisition program, rather than a document-access program. The plan was discontinued at the end of 1972.

shared pool, or by the reproduction of specific titles upon demand.

With some important exceptions, existing systems of sharing resources that depend upon decentralized sharing in more or less conventional ways through lending from one library to another have not seemed overwhelmingly successful. The true costs are high, the speed is relatively slow, the location of wanted material is often uncertain, and the assurance of access, even when the location is known, is also uncertain. These factors combine to impede the kinds of intellectual or creative interaction that may occur when there is more rapid access, or the assurance of access within a specified time. The ability to browse tends to be sacrificed in most such systems, but the values associated with browsing in collections of this kind may be small in relation to the probable costs. Such benefits as may attach to browsing might also reflect, in part, deficiencies in the existing bibliographical apparatus.

The direct costs of access in most of the existing decentralized systems tend to fall at present more heavily on the lender than on the borrower. The existing interlibrary loan system could clearly be strengthened by more formal contractual relationships, by more equitable cost allocations, by teletype request for needed material, by reduced red tape in loans, by faster and lower-cost photocopying (where possible), by clearing-house fiscal settlements, by the better prior verification of desired items, and by the creation of a more inclusive and current record of the holdings of all participating institutions—with the record widely available to all potential borrowers. Not all of these conditions are likely to be met, and the adverse experience of many users with existing systems of interlibrary loan, combined with anxieties about the intellectual losses from the inability to have quick access and the opportunity to browse, have tended to inhibit the development of effective alternative systems. Furthermore, it is not unknown for an institution to attach prestige, as well as functional, values to the size of its library.

The present systems of decentralized access to informally shared resources thus have two major sets of defects: (1) they do not offer constructive encouragement to a participating institution to reduce its own acquisitions, with the knowledge that unpurchased materials will, in fact, be available; and (2) the reliability, costs, assurance of access, bibliographical control, and speed of the alternative systems are poor, even for materials known to be held and, theoretically, available.

The possibility of limiting acquisitions in a single institution—were good alternative means of access available—is critically important because of the potential savings in (1) the initial costs of acquisition, (2) the associated processing costs, (3) the space costs required to house the materials, and (4) the relatively high cost/benefit ratios associated with much of the material that is now acquired (or sought) by a large research library. For many voluminous types of material the costs of local acquisition and retention may be very high and the frequency of use, very low. This results, of course, in very high unit use costs when these costs are computed on the basis of actual or average use.

These costs are so high, in fact, that the investment of a portion of the required funds in other means of access might in the long run be more rewarding if the most infrequently used materials could easily be made available when needed. Obviously the historical and humanistic disciplines are most dependent upon infrequently used materials. Both librarians and scholars have come, perhaps quite naturally, to substitute as a library objective book acquisitions and *holdings* rather than book or information *access*. In terms of functions and costs they are clearly different. Obviously there are complex issues here of primary versus secondary materials, standards of quality, the research use of ephemeral or popular publications, and other related distinctions.

It is evident that some system for the decentralized sharing of responsibility among institutions by subject, language, geographic origin, and so forth, will need to continue for the bulk of retrospective imprints that are now held by major scholarly libraries [48]. It is most unrealistic to assume that the present holdings of Yale, Harvard, or the British Museum, for example, could be duplicated for the purpose of establishing a central shared-resources pool. There could at best be only partial duplication by means of limited, or highly selective, photocopying. What is probably needed in terms of access to large bodies of retrospective materials is essentially equitable cost sharing of loan services, efficient loan procedures, excellent bibliographical control, and, possibly, some photocopying of materials of major, general significance.

However, a decentralized system of sharing those retrospective resources already held in major libraries does not provide an optimum pattern on which to build an effective system for the long-term future development of shared resource access except (1) where the close physical proximity of two or more institutions substantially meets the basic conditions outlined above, or (2) the subject field is very highly specialized and of very limited general concern, for example, Icelandic literature. The reasons, resummarized, are: (1) Such systems will continue to offer relatively slower, less certain, and more costly means of access. (2) They are likely to continue to be sufficiently unreliable so that local acquisitions are unlikely to be significantly reduced. (3) The "owning" institution will almost always seem to be deriving some kind of preferential access priorities or benefits for its local constituency as compared with other users. (4) It will not be feasible to divide responsibility for substantial bodies of literature, for instance, many serials, without heavy redundancy or rather arbitrary language or geographic divisions. (5) The concept of national centers of excellence with federal funding will prove politically unattractive, for it will seem to make the rich, richer and the poor, poorer. (6) Academic competition will make the "centers of excellence" approach unacceptable to distinguished scholars except for those whose subject interests coincide with the collecting responsibilities of their own institutions.[19] (7) Local subject priorities shift with time, and as they shift, local acquisition priorities inevitably will, or should, be altered. And (8) equitable cost allocation is difficult in such an environment, and hence external funding will be difficult to administer. Under the stimulus of federal aid, state-oriented systems of compensation for decentralized shared access are emerging. It can be argued that many of these state systems are likely to prove unduly expensive or inadequate for many needs at the *research level* in comparison with either national or quite large regional systems.

The design of shared-access systems should be shaped by a variety of carefully chosen priorities that will have the combined effect of maximizing the total body of resources; the speed of access, especially to the more frequently used materials; the assurance of access; and the size of the population to be served. These objectives should be coupled with that of minimizing the aggregate costs of the system. Thus the priorities for acquisition in a national resource pool might take the following order: (1) newly appearing serial titles; (2) other serial titles, beginning with those believed to be less frequently used and in foreign languages; (3) current monographs, initially selected on the basis of country of publication and language, possibly leaving English-language publications to the last on the assumption that they already may be the most widely available and most heavily used; (4) current English-language monographs; (5) runs of retrospective serials received by gift; and (6) retrospective monographs received by gift. The high priority attached to serials is based upon the facts that (1) serial costs tend to become a permanent prior lien on library acquisition funds (plus space, plus binding, plus processing); (2) selection, once made, does not have to be repeated to sustain the resource pool and a high level of expenditures for acquisition purposes; (3) bibliographical control of many serial publications is provided by locally available indexing, citation, and abstracting services; (4) serials tend to be important to many aspects of scholarship; and (5) the high inflation in serial costs in recent years could make the fiscal leverage of such access relatively significant.

---

[19]This is a rather critical point. Two scholars of equal distinction working in the same field will be willing, under some circumstances, to share in the use of an infrequently used body of material located in a "neutral" pool where the arrangements for access are more or less equal. By contrast, a dependence on key source materials from a "center of excellence" located in one academic institution will lead the scholars in other institutions to be exceedingly restless until their local libraries have attained full parity. What self-respecting scholar would want to work, by inference at least, in a center of nonexcellence in his own field? If federal support of such centers were to be limited strictly to the direct costs of service to external users, the competitive pressures would be reduced, but the quality of access is still likely to be unsatisfactory. Alternatively, if centers of excellence were to mean the development of duplicative, more or less comprehensive collections on a regional basis, without preferential benefits to a single institution, there would be less difficulty, but the need for such duplication of resources in terms of frequency of use probably does not exist.

A central resource pool or pools, depending upon location, would tend to neutralize needless institutional competition in a constructive way; might be very helpful in reducing geographic and institutional inequities; could result in substantial reductions in local duplicative acquisitions; would clearly identify access and use costs; would be relatively less affected by many local changes in policies or fiscal resources; would be specifically geared to high-speed, relatively reliable service; and would moderate the growth pressures on acquisition budgets as well as the associated processing, space, and overhead costs. Such a central pool should be able to alert potential users to its resources more easily than a highly decentralized system of resources.

Perhaps the best model of such a central pool of resources with many of these characteristics is the National Lending Library for Science and Technology in England. This seems to be a well-conceived and economical solution to a set of critical resource problems. It almost certainly has the lowest unit access costs of any major research literature-access system. In terms of the size and corpus of the literature available, it may well be the fastest and most reliable such system in operation. The National Lending Library (NLL) is now loaning, by photocopy or by original issue, between 3,000–4,000 items per day and is receiving around 40,000 current serial titles. The initial concentration was on the serial literature of science and technology. The library is now beginning to collect in the social sciences.

England is much smaller than the United States; the mail service is incomparably superior; the NLL enjoys advantageous fair-use copyright legislation that permits the effective use of photocopying under appropriate limitations, mail franking privileges, and government funding. These elements may be difficult to achieve to the same degree in this country, but these differences do not seem of a character to argue that the NLL concept is invalid. There is some tendency to say that an NLL in this country would be welcome if federally funded. That would obviously be both desirable and an efficient means of federal support of research libraries and research, but it may be both necessary and feasible for libraries to reallocate their present resources in such a way as to support such a system—perhaps excluding space costs. Progress would certainly be slower under these circumstances. However, a very crude and unverified estimate suggests that the ARL libraries alone may presently be spending as much as $33 million a year on serials, serial binding, and serial processing. This is a sum sufficiently large to suggest the feasibility of a significant joint program with a rather modest reallocation of resources if many institutions were to share in the enterprise.

The classical objections will include the loss of browsing, anxieties about the ease or assurance of access to such a pool, the economic threat to the survival of certain publications that have a marginal economic existence at the present time, and uncertainty about the scope of fair use under the present copyright act with respect to photocopying. It should be noted that one cannot browse in a journal that is not available; that there are many journal items in which browsing is not necessary and in which it is probably very rare; that, if a pooled-access system is sufficiently efficient, one may obtain certain "possibly relevant" publications for browsing purposes from a pool, recognizing that not all will be useful. Possible copyright restraints on photocopying are not insuperable obstacles. If fair use by means of photocopying cannot be reflected in legislation or by judicial precedent, then such a center could loan the original publications. In some instances it might be advantageous for a center to subscribe to more than one copy of a journal and thus be able to loan either whole issues or individual articles. Those journals that are very infrequently used, yet totally dependent upon library subscriptions, may need to adopt alternative methods of publication and distribution; such alternatives exist. There is a serious question as to whether library budgets are the appropriate or the best means of supporting scholarly journals. The increasing number of subscription rates that are significantly higher for libraries than for individuals, for the same journal, may accelerate the development of shared-access systems. It should also be noted that thousands of serials received by libraries are of a professional, governmental, trade, or popular nature, and are not significantly dependent upon the library market. There seems to be very persuasive evidence in the British experience to support the early establishment of such an enterprise in this country and to broaden its scope as rapidly as possible. Such a facility should increase the aggregate resource base and should, more gradually perhaps, begin to improve the cost/effectiveness ratio of resource access.

The Center for Research Libraries, located in Chicago, is in some respects such an enterprise. It is a separate, not-for-profit corporation with more than fifty full-member institutions and some thirty associate members. It offers to its members two basic services in terms of shared resource access. In its initial years it offered to receive, retain a single copy of, and make available to its members research materials no longer required by a participating institution. The potential economy here is not so much in the local saving of space as in the extension of the resource base available to all members from the deposit of a title, coupled with the fact that any member institution could, given the assurance of future access to a title at the Center, discard, if it wished, any locally held duplicate copies. More significantly, the Center has also engaged in the large-scale acquisition of certain well-defined bodies of infrequently used research material for the joint benefit of its member institutions. Examples include a wide variety of microform archives, all the current and retrospective publications of the Soviet Academy of Sciences, current subscriptions to some 7,000 infrequently used scientific journals,[20]

---

[20]This program is being expanded in 1973 as the result of a substantial grant from the Carnegie Corporation.

any foreign or domestic doctoral dissertation requested by a member, the documents of the fifty states, etc. This collective mode of acquisition and sharing of resources is clearly a source of very large potential savings in the acquisition costs of any individual institutional member. The Center, given the wide spectrum of resources that it acquires on behalf of its members, has at least three problems: (1) One cannot be sure that the individual reader in a member institution knows of the resources available in the Center, despite special printed catalogs and bibliographies that the Center has issued. (2) The Center is in urgent need of space. Its original building, given through grants from the Carnegie Corporation and the Rockefeller Foundation, is essentially full (in excess of 3 million volume equivalents), and rented space is now being used. (3) There are still many librarians—and faculty members—who tend to compute the cost/benefit ratio of Center membership by dividing the annual membership fee[21] by the number of items requested on loan during a given year. This calculation fails to recognize that the annual membership fee purchases a *right of access* to a very large body of materials that, by definition, is likely to be infrequently used. The acquisition expenditures of the Center in some recent years, with the aid of substantial federal grants, have ranged from $250,000 to more than $350,000 in 1970-71. The method of measuring benefits, described above, is not commonly applied by scholars or librarians to the costs of locally acquired, infrequently used resources.

The concepts of both the Center for Research Libraries and the National Lending Library offer large potentials for sharp improvement in the cost/effectiveness relationships for many kinds of infrequently used scholarly materials. Neither can take the place of basic, locally available, research collections and materials that are frequently used and material of substantial scholarly importance in fields that are of enduring, major, institutional interest, regardless of the frequency of use. It is extremely important to recognize that there will be few or no absolute criteria—for example, frequency of use—for determining whether research materials should be held locally or in a shared pool. These criteria and determinations will have to be made in terms of the cost effectiveness of the alternative systems of access. If a shared-access system is highly effective in terms of user access and costs, it can reduce the relative need for locally held resources. If the shared system is ineffective, it will be unlikely to reduce the pressures for local collection development regardless of cost.

However, if the local collection, despite rising costs, continues to be inadequate in scope in relation to many users' needs, or if the library's bibliographical and other services are, or seem to be, basically inefficient, or otherwise unresponsive, or if the library system simply requires a reader

---

[21]Depending upon the expenditures of the member library and other factors, the full-membership fee ranged from $4,620 to $16,493 in 1971-72.

effort that seems disproportionate to the benefits, alternative systems of bibliographical control, data access, and literature access are likely to be encouraged, especially for portions of the high-use, current literature. These alternative systems may, in some aspects, be essentially independent of the library and, taken in the aggregate, much more costly than would be the case if the overall, library-based, bibliographical-, literature-, and data-access systems were strengthened.

PHOTOCOPYING

Within certain limits, it is now theoretically feasible for a library or an individual reader to secure from the holdings of another library a photocopy of a manuscript, an article, a portion of a book, an entire volume, or a major collection. The photocopy can be made from the original at the time of the request, or it can be quickly duplicated from a master photocopy negative of the original if one has previously been made and retained by the library holding the originals or by some other institution. The technologies in common use are roll microfilms, microfiche, and electrostatic, paper photocopies. Given these means of access, it is evident that a rather powerful shared-access mechanism exists in which the resource base is, in effect, the aggregate of the resources of all libraries willing to participate in such a system.

Very extensive use is, in fact, being made of this system of access, but it suffers from a number of limitations. Among these are the following: (1) There may often be very substantial delays before copies can be made and received. (2) Not all libraries have adequate technical facilities to produce photocopies of high quality at low costs. (3) Some libraries may be unwilling to supply photocopies of certain holdings. (4) Some libraries believe that in some circumstances partial compensation should be paid to the owning library for the initial costs of acquisition and processing of the desired material, especially in those cases where the materials are rare, costly, or unusual. (5) The desired materials may be too fragile or bound too tightly to permit satisfactory photocopying. (6) The desired materials may be in use and the local library may be reluctant to recall them or may be able to secure their return only after a long delay. (7) The costs are not negligible—they may approximate five to ten cents a page for a negative microfilm and ten to twenty cents a page for a full-size photocopy. (8) Users are generally unenthusiastic about microform copies (if given a choice of originals or full-size copies). (9) The copyright law does not permit the photocopying, without permission, of extensive portions or complete, copyrighted works. (10) The more limited extract photocopying from copyrighted publications, under the fair-use concept of the copyright law, is presently in dispute.

Although very significant use is being made of microforms and full-size photocopying, the restraints or limitations listed above may explain, in part, why these technologies thus far seem to have fallen somewhat short of their theoretical potential and why the more traditional concepts of academic collection development have been relatively little affected. These matters would seem to deserve further attention.

The widespread utilization of electrostatic photocopying processes has greatly facilitated the exchange of information among investigators prior to formal publication; greatly reduced the burdens of note taking and manual transcription in assembling, from locally available materials, the data required by students and scholars alike in the preparation of reports and papers; and made it possible for investigators to secure periodical articles and other similar research materials from distant libraries or repositories in a convenient form and at reasonable costs. Where such equipment is readily available and the costs seem reasonable, it has probably reduced the theft and mutilation of library-owned publications. For limited bodies of materials the costs have been acceptable, and the form and quality of the reproduction have usually been satisfactory to users, except where accurate reproduction of color, photographs, or half-tones is required. The availability of the electrostatic full-size copying processes has, to a large extent, superseded the former use of microfilm for the reproduction of short-run or smaller quantities of material, for example, a copy of a journal article. The product is obviously far easier to use and is not, in short runs, appreciably more costly.

Microforms, in consequence, have tended in recent years to be used for the on-demand reproduction of longer runs of material, that is, full volumes or multivolume sets; for the preservation of originals printed on poor paper; as a primary or alternative means of original publication (often with full-size electrostatic prints as an alternative product); as a means for the sale or distribution of long-runs of material or of specially selected collections of retrospective materials; and as a means of securing permanent or archival copies of newspapers and certain serial publications.

The patterns for the production and sale or distribution of microforms have been exceptionally complex and have included: (1) the on-demand reproduction by one library for another or for an individual; (2) the same procedure except that the owning library retains a master negative of the desired film, making a positive copy for which the original requestor may or may not be asked to bear the costs; (3) the organization by a single library or a group of libraries of a special microfilming project, the costs of which are equally shared; (4) the offering by a commercial firm of a microform collection, based upon original publications or manuscripts which may be located in one or several different libraries; (5) licensing of commercial agencies by a few libraries to microfilm resources with the understanding that the owning library will receive a royalty on all sales; (6) subscription, through the publisher or through an agent designated by the publisher, to microfilm copies of many current and retrospective newspaper files and serials; (7) purchasing of microfilm copies of doctoral theses accepted by most U.S. universities from a commercial organization; etc.

It should be noted that once a master negative microform has been made, there is the theoretical possibility that such an item will always be "in print." Thus one could, under the right system, always procure copies either by loan or by purchase at the time of demand. Although this is true, it has been a common practice for institutions and commercial microform producers alike to develop multicopy duplication projects—essentially in a pattern similar to that used in original or reprint publishing. The simultaneous sale of copies to a number of subscribers makes it easy to amortize the initial cost of the negative film. There has, until recently, been relatively little original publication in microform, the bulk of the work thus being "reprints" of materials that originally appeared in conventionally printed forms.

The introduction of the microfiche has, for some purposes, made the manipulation of microforms simpler for the user than was the case with roll film. A number of relatively large-scale systems of document access have coupled a printed abstract or bibliographical service and the original distribution of the cited text in either microfiche or a full-size print, for example, the ERIC system (Educational Resources Information Center) or the NTIS system (National Technical Information Service) for technical report literature. Such systems offer potentially economical and efficient access to important bodies of material at relatively low costs. The direct coupling of bibliographical and document access, if associated with high-speed services and low document costs, offers the user an effective, integrated capability. These services, thus far, are largely institutionally oriented, but there is no reason why they could not be shaped to meet the needs of individuals or disciplinary groups. The American Institute of Physics has moved in this direction, and there are related developments in other areas.

A successful instance of a microform system of shared resources is the Association of Research Libraries' project for current foreign newspapers. In this plan, the Center for Research Libraries collects current foreign newspapers and has them microfilmed, or simply subscribes to microfilm copies where such are available. Participating institutions pay a project membership fee of approximately $785 per year. The fee enables the member to borrow microfilm prints of any available title at any time, and to purchase microfilm prints, if desired, at the cost of the positive. The pool of available newpapers has over a long period of years become a large one, the participation costs to a single institution are very modest in relation to the costs of acquiring such a body of material unilaterally, and access is reliable and reasonably fast.

One major microform publisher has for some years offered subscriptions at rather reasonable costs for a substantial number of periodical titles in roll microform to those libraries that also subscribe to the originals. The argument is that the microform avoids the costs of binding the originals, eliminates the need to replace missing issues, and reduces space requirements. The principal objection is that consultation is more difficult than is the case with originals.

Microform technology has many theoretical benefits that have been exploited for a number of major uses, but it has never seemed to fulfill its full potential. Trends at the moment seem mixed. On the one hand, there has been an entry into the field of several large organizations with substantial capital resources, a number of new technologies, and ambitions to use microform technology for very large-scale republishing. In contrast to these trends, it must be noted that the industry has failed to standardize its product. The proliferation of new sizes of transparencies and opaques, with different reduction ratios, each system requiring its own reading equipment, and often with indifferent product quality control, has posed very serious difficulties for libraries, and has resulted in virtually no interest on the part of individuals in purchasing reading equipment or microforms. There is recent evidence of a trend toward greater standardization in reduction ratios, image size, and format.[22] This could be very advantageous to libraries in terms of the efficiency of equipment utilization and quality control.

At least three firms in recent years have brought out high-reduction systems in which reduction ratios have ranged from 55:1 to 150:1. The use of high reduction ratios obviously reduces the amount of sensitive material required for printing a copy or an edition. However, the high-reduction processes normally require a two-step optical reduction process to generate the master negative. This can be an expensive process with little leeway for error. The size of the edition required to make such high-reduction processes economically competitive with the lower-reduction-ratio processes may fall between 150 and 500 copies. Such an edition size may in some cases be larger than the current potential market for copies. The cost, per copy, of the lower-reduction microfiche and roll film processes becomes nearly linear after a relatively small run or edition, that is, around fifteen to twenty copies. Adequate reading equipment and the equipment needed for making full-size paper enlargements are both likely to be less costly for moderate reduction materials. Very high reduction materials probably cannot be easily replicated locally on a one-for-one reduction-ratio basis.

Several proposals have been made in recent years to create and distribute microform "libraries" of, say, 1 million volumes, for example, the Rand Corporation memorandum of 1968 [25]. Library Resources, Inc., and National Cash Register[23] have offered large "packages" or collections of reproduced works. Such undertakings could make available, in time, collections that

---

[22] I am indebted to Carl Spaulding for recent information on standardization and several related matters in the microphotographic field. A brief, but useful, general review of the microform field has recently been made by Spigai [47].

[23] It is understood that the National Cash Register Co. plans to withdraw from this field.

would now be unattainable in original form. However, such collections thus far have avoided the inclusion of copyrighted materials. The primary need of the relatively small college library may be for recent copyrighted books and journals. The very large research libraries, on the other hand, may be reluctant to accept the implied duplication in large "package" approaches. The costs for the packages are not negligible, though substantially less than the costs for the original publications if available.

With such collections, the question clearly arises as to whether functional requirements could equally well be met by a central pool of one positive set of prints from which loans could be made or a master set of negatives from which copies could be printed on demand. This is primarily a problem of cost determination, amortization of capital investment, copyright issues, demand, and the values to be attached to immediate access. It should be noted that single diazo copies made, on demand, from moderate-reduction and low-reduction microfiche can probably be produced at costs lower than the costs for the loan of a book to an individual in the typical library.

A variety of business-oriented systems to retrieve selected microform images from a microfilm roll or a larger microform "store" in response to a keyed or programmed search, and to display or print out the text quickly, are now operational. However, most of these systems involve relatively high access costs and probably cannot be justified in a library at the present time. They would become applicable only where use was exceptionally heavy and file integrity was critically important.[24]

There is a substantial potential for microfilm technology in terms of preservation and assured access to infrequently used resources at relatively low costs. The technique has been important in preservation, critically essential in the use of newpapers, and has made a very substantial amount of other material available to many libraries. The technology seems on balance under utilized as the result of readers' general dissatisfaction with the technology because of the poor design of much reading equipment, frequently poor quality control in products, failure to standardize with resulting high costs for equipment and equipment maintenance, often very poor environmental conditions for use in libraries, and failure to build a personal market.

A key problem with the use of microforms in scholarship relates to the difficulty of consulting many different pages, references, or sections from different works as one writes a paper or engages in other typical scholarly work. The technology has also been handicapped by the general absence of a system in which the user may easily go from full-size materials to microforms, microform master to microform copy, and microform to full-size copy. The space savings have not been sufficiently attractive from a cost-reduction point of view to induce academic institutions to use the technology for that

---

[24]Many of these devices and other microphotographic equipment are described in Ballou [6].

purpose alone. A single institution can usually build added space in which to house books at lower costs than it can *initially* microfilm the originals. There are differences in views on the role of the commercial entrepreneur in a field in which the materials come primarily from libraries and the products are sold almost entirely to libraries.

The combination of a better standardized microform technology with (1) a capability for making low-cost, reliable, semiautomatic, full-size printouts on demand;[25] (2) the availability of highly reliable and comfortable reading devices, at costs low enough to appeal to individuals as well as to institutions; (3) a capability by means of which an individual or an institution could make compatible microforms easily, inexpensively, and quickly; and (4) a technology in which institutions could print copies of microforms on demand at extremely low costs, could offer a relatively powerful system in terms of a broad spectrum of information access and use requirements. A change in the concepts of journal distribution to a microform format in which articles, rather than journal issues, were the basic units might also be important if the "articles" could be distributed to match the interests of an individual.

This review has not attempted to examine the permanence of film or color images, or the effect of different reduction ratios on image quality. Many of these points have been dealt with extensively in the literature.

Microform and computer technology have, within the last few years, been coupled to form an essentially new and potentially very powerful capability in COM (computer output microform). This technology provides for the optical formation, by means of a computer, of characters which are then recorded at extremely high speeds on microfilm, usually from a magnetic tape in a batch-mode output. The technology can work with very large computer data bases, can reduce the computer time normally used for conventional output printing, can provide printouts at very high speeds, and can provide very large and complex character sets, limited essentially only by input coding restraints or difficulties. The costs of such outputs are relatively low. This technology could be extremely valuable in generating library catalogs, union lists, bibliographies, and other useful outputs. The technology is now in use as a replacement for the card catalog in several libraries in England. It eliminates all manual filing, provides for the inexpensive duplication of complete catalogs, appears to be acceptable to users, and reduces costs [13, 31, 49]. Other technologies are already available that can make full-size paper prints, offset printing plates, or other products from microform when required.

---

[25]The Xerox Corporation is understood to be working on such a capability for microfiche. There is already available, of course, large-scale production equipment for such printouts from roll microfilm.

FACSIMILE TRANSMISSION

Obviously, facsimile transmission is a communication device and could be discussed under such a heading. It is, at the same time, a technology that, in theory, could make the resources of one library available elsewhere with, it would seem, little delay. It is for this reason that it is treated here as an aspect of making shared resources available.

A number of libraries have experimented with facsimile transmission of textual materials. To the best of my knowledge all of these test operations have subsequently been abandoned. The reasons are relatively clear. Facsimile technology permits the transfer, by telephone circuit, cable, or microwave circuit, of textual material from one library to another; the technology is improving, Its practical utility depends, however, on the performance of facsimile as part of a larger system, for example: (1) the time required and the costs of making the original request, (2) the time and costs of getting the wanted material to a facsimile transmitting facility in the owning library, (3) the time and cost for making the single-sheet photocopy of the wanted material that is presently typically required for low-cost scanning purposes, (4) the actual transmission time and costs, (5) the pro rata cost of the scanning and receiving equipment, (6) the image quality of the products, (7) the time required to place the transmitted copy in the hands of the user at the receiving end of the system, and (8) a relatively smooth demand curve.

There are facsimile systems of high capacity and relatively high image quality. Such systems have relatively high band-width requirements—for example, coaxial cables—and the costs of the scanning and receiving equipment are such that a high volume of sustained traffic is required to attain acceptable unit cost levels. Low-cost terminals, and narrow-band-width circuitry,—for example, ordinary telephone circuits—result in relatively low equipment costs, slow transmissions, and thus very limited capacity and relatively high unit costs. The delays in locating desired items in the transmitting library, in preparing the copy for transmission, and in the transmission time itself, all combine in such a way that a reader is unlikely to want to wait at a receiving terminal the several hours (or days) that may be needed. He may thus not return for his material until the next day. Under these circumstances a photocopy sent by mail may be less costly and equally satisfactory. Facsimile costs have been relatively high, that is, several times the unit costs of, say, a Xerox copy sent by air mail. Performance might be improved in some cases by transmission between regional centers to maximize loads and thus reduce the unit costs of wide-band circuitry. However, it is doubtful that for most scholarly needs a strong case can be made for general facsimile transmission of text until such time as costs are significantly lower, capacity is higher, equipment for transmitting directly from bound volumes is available, and image quality is higher. Obviously a collection of noncirculating microforms may form a more suitable corpus for use as a source for facsimile transmission of textual materials, but again one must examine the logical, if more pedestrian, economic and functional alternatives of high-speed microform replication and the mailing of wanted items or of mass replication and distribution of suitable packages of microforms in anticipation of future needs.

It is also feasible to tranfer by wire, cable, or microwave circuitry, textual materials that have been converted into digital form and stored in computer-controlled devices. Except for relatively limited bodies of material, likely to be subjected to high-frequency use, the present costs of such storage and transmission for large bodies of textual materials are too high to make the technology seem attractive in comparison with the performance of lower-cost, but slower, alternative means of access. It is important, as in all assessments of technology, to examine with care the functional requirements, the costs, and the alternative solutions. At the present time, the large-scale transfer of textual data, of the kind commonly stored in books and journals, by means of facsimile transmission or by means of digital conversion, storage, and transmission, appears to be relatively unattractive, primarily from an economic point of view but also because of some functional or qualitative limitations. However, the long-term technological and related potentials for altered and improved systems of data or literature transfer and access are substantial. Such potentials might be realized rather quickly, for example, if heavily subsidized access to wide-band circuitry were to become readily available to libraries, for example, via CATV systems, educational microwave networks, or other channels. Furthermore it is important to distinguish between the utility of remote access to computer-stored bibliographical and factual data, and "conventional" bodies of textual data or literature.

Nontechnical references on several aspects of facsimile transmission and many related issues will be found in [9, 16, 26].

COPYRIGHT

The present U.S. statutes on copyright do not permit the reproduction of materials protected by an unexpired copyright claim without the permission of the copyright owner. Under the concept of "fair use" it has been assumed, through long customary usage, that the making of a photocopy of a limited portion of a larger work, for example, an article from a serial publication, fell within the legitimate scope of fair use, as a substitute for the normal transcription of such material [15].

A recent opinion by a hearing commissioner of the U.S. Court of Claims [56] challenges the long-established assumption that the making of a single photocopy of a single article or a small segment of a larger work, in response to a specific request from a reader, in lieu of manual transcription, represents a "fair use" of copyrighted materials. This case has now been argued before the full Court of Claims, but a decision has not been announced at this writing. There are assumptions that any decision is likely to be appealed to the U.S. Supreme Court. The case grows out of a suit by a publisher of a number of medical journals against the National Library of Medicine, which has developed and sponsored a large-scale, national, medical-literature-access system, involving both bibiographical analysis and document or resource access. A number of detailed studies have been made of the actual photocopying practices undertaken in a number of the larger scholarly libraries in the United States and Canada. These studies do not seem to reflect photocopying practices that are in violation of the "fair use" concept of the law, nor do they seem to threaten or impair the economic benefits enjoyed by a publisher under copyright [23, 50]. However, these views are not now accepted by a portion of the publishing industry which sees a serious economic threat in the growing ease of photocopying. By way of contrast, the copyright act of 1956 of the United Kingdom provides very explicitly for the limited photocopying of copyrighted materials if in compliance with a number of very reasonable limitations.

The technology of relatively fast and inexpensive reproduction of limited bodies of research material is an important aspect of research literature and information access. The protection of such access may require a suitable amendment to the U.S. copyright act defining "fair use."

CONCLUSION

The electrostatic, full-size copying techniques have, in a relatively short period of time, become very important tools in many aspects of scholarly work. This technology could easily become a powerful means for short-run or on-demand publication. The technology in an effective combination with microform may offer even greater benefits.

Microform technologies, including roll, cassette, microfiche, and other variants, have been of substantial scholarly importance with respect to preservation and access to large collections and other bodies of material not otherwise available. Even so, for many reasons the technology is not commonly viewed with affection by most users. The development of a well-designed, complete microform system, that had sufficient appeal to both individual and institutional users, could bring about a significant change. There is now significantly more commercial interest in microform "publishing" than in the past. Much of the current commercial utilization of microforms is for in-house industrial and commercial use, for example, parts catalogs, archival records, etc. The potential of COM (computer output microform) may be very great, especially for bibliographical tools.

Facsimile transmission of textual materials has not thus far seemed, on balance, a cost-effective literature-access technology. The ready availability of wide-band channels at very low costs could alter the situation.

CHAPTER 4

This entire field is one in which there always is, or at least seems to be, a prospect for significant technological change. For example, video disks are said to have extremely high information capacities at very low duplicative costs; holography is also said to offer somewhat similar possibilities; there are a variety of other proposals for storing and transferring large masses of data. Such information storage or processing possibilities are clearly of potential significance to the library and its users. Even with major new capabilities, however, there would be substantial conversion costs for retrospective materials. It is worth noting that the printed book or page is still, for many uses, a singularly efficient and attractive technology.

5

THE COMPUTER AND THE LIBRARY

The growth of the literature, the increasing volume of research work and graduate study, the growing dependence of modern society on relevant information, the emergence of new kinds of mission- and discipline-oriented bibliographical and information systems, the widespread (though perhaps not always fully justified) criticisms of, or dissatisfactions with current information-access capabilities and processes, coupled with the visible problems, costs, and other restraints of existing library systems, lead to a number of conclusions: (1) better information-access mechanisms are desired; (2) such improved access systems may be economically and intellectually important to society and scholarship; (3) major improvements in access are unlikely to occur as the result of simple extensions of existing systems or operations—indeed, the reverse may be true; (4) through the wise utilization of technology and other measures, improvements in information systems within reasonable economic limitations seem feasible; and (5) technology alone is unlikely to solve all the problems, including those of an economic and intellectual nature.

The basic case for the use of technology, and especially for the use of computers, as a means of improving access to recorded knowledge and information has been made by many observers, including Vannevar Bush in 1945. The case for such utilization rests primarily upon the following circumstances: (1) The library and its users are critically dependent upon very large, very complex, file-structured data bases that are required for operational and bibliographical purposes. (2) There is growing recognition that these large, file-oriented data bases are increasingly inflexible in their manual form as a consequence of sheer size and related complexity. (3) The files are very expensive to create and to maintain, yet they may be relatively inefficient in responding to many user and operational needs. (4) There are seasonal and other uneven library work-load problems that are not readily compatible with manually operated systems. (5) The labor-intensive nature of library operations—with a high percentage of all labor costs directly involved in the many repetitive tasks associated with creating, maintaining, changing, updating and otherwise using file-oriented data—tends to force increasingly higher average unit and marginal costs that will tend to rise more rapidly than general cost indexes or tax revenues. (6) Many of the decision-making processes related to the use of library files are highly formal, and decisions can often be determined by formal rules based upon the status of file data. (7) Existing systems for handling such data provide extremely meager and otherwise unsatisfactory performance data on the system.

The theoretical potential of the computer in this context has also been sufficiently well stated by many others and requires here only the most abridged summary. The computer has the capacity to store large data files; to order and maintain such files; to add, delete, alter, and extend file data; to search; to create new files or subfiles from available data; to monitor loads and system performance; to generate a wide array of outputs in terms of formats, data content, arrangement, and speed of access. The trends of computer unit processing costs, speeds, and capacities are all favorable in contrast to each of these factors in manually based data-processing systems.

The widely used term "library automation" is somewhat misleading. What is basically involved can be roughly categorized as data-processing functions, data-retrieval functions, and the generation and retrieval of performance data in the broad management sense of systems performance. The operational, processing, bibliographical, and performance data are critically interrelated. The data structures and the means of data access are important both to users, in their efforts to identify and secure access to relevant literature and information, and to libraries in an operational sense.

It is evident that there are some obstacles. For example, there are still serious technical and intellectual problems in connection with computer-based organization, maintenance, and searching of extremely large files; library applications require extremely large storage capacities at reasonably low storage and access costs because much of the data is infrequently used; many of the existing input and output terminal devices and methodologies are not entirely satisfactory for many library needs, for example, character-font size, cost, speed, noise, etc.; computer costs for some existing library applications have been higher than the superseded manual processes; and there have often been more difficult system design and development problems than were initially anticipated.

Detailed breakdowns of costs for existing library processes are themselves costly and quite difficult to obtain, usually requiring many assumptions or arbitrary cost distributions for shared processes, the maintenance of shared data bases, and other factors. The costs of computer-based systems are in most library applications even more difficult to allocate to specific functions except in those few instances where products and processes, before and after, are essentially the same. There have been relatively high developmental costs for new systems, and the methods of distributing these costs present obvious difficulties. There are wide variations in the algorithms for allocating institutional computer costs, and these are subject to frequent alteration within many institutions. The more careful studies related to costs of operating computer-based, library data-processing or access systems have not generally promised significant *initial* cost reductions (e.g. [22, 30, 46]).

The use of computers in the library has been challenged for one or more of the following reasons: cost savings have not been achieved, cost savings are not in prospect, or operating performance will not be significantly improved by means of such technologies—at least within prospective levels of library support (e.g. [36, 37]). Stanford University concluded, in one of the most detailed studies of the prospective use of a complex system for computer-based data processing, that "the cost of automation to Stanford is high and savings will be non-existent in the next few years" [58]. The Stanford prediction of long-term future savings is therefore predicated upon a number of rather uncertain assumptions about future cost trends and loads. The Stanford arguments in behalf of proceeding to develop a major computer-based system were thus based primarily upon improved library performance. The Stanford system is designed to utilize a very large computer system in an on-line mode with a very large data base. The Systems Staff of the University of Chicago Library has projected significant cost savings and performance improvements within a two- to four-year period after large-scale implementation with a relatively large system offering both batch and on-line capabilities to be utilized in technical processing, circulation, and other operations. Thus far, virtually all cost calculations for the larger, more or less integrated systems have excluded the design and developmental costs to bring up the initial system. The design and development of initial systems is expensive and difficult. Once accomplished, however, similar capabilities can be replicated or developed, at very much lower cost and with relatively high assurance of success.

Obviously if the initial operating costs of computer-based systems are significantly higher than the superseded manual processes, if the operational costs of such systems are trending down very slowly, if the developmental costs are high, if the load of work is essentially constant, and if the immediate or long-term performance of the overall library system will be essentially unchanged, there is no argument for mechanization. These factors are not inevitably applicable to all machine-based systems and some are simply untrue. It is clear that large, complex, versatile, computer-based, library data-processing systems are costly to develop. This is partly due to the complexity of the requirements, and partly to the pioneering nature of the effort. Money has undoubtedly been wasted on some ill-conceived or badly executed library projects. This has also been true of efforts to use large-scale computer technology in business, industry, and government. A complex new technology can rarely be applied without taking some risks and making some errors. However, research and developmental funds for technological innovation in libraries are so extremely limited that unusually thoughtful and perceptive planning is required to minimize, insofar as possible, the high risks associated with such developmental efforts. It is neither economically feasible nor functionally required that every library build its own major data-processing capability, and methods for developing "standard-package" or joint library data-processing capabilities are clearly needed and in prospect. It is also important to note the observations in prior chapters that point to unacceptable increases in costs and the gradual degradation of services unless ameliorative steps are taken.

In terms of operating costs for smaller systems using new technologies, there are indications, despite meager and unsatisfactory data, that some single-process-oriented data-processing applications (e.g., circulation) have reduced unit costs—sometimes, however, with certain offsetting reductions in some aspects of performance. Reasonably comprehensive, highly integrated, multipurpose systems may easily generate initial unit costs somewhat higher than manual costs for the same outputs. Costs will depend upon the efficiency of the system design; the nature of the functions to be performed; the modes of access to the data; the institutional algorithms for allocating computer costs; whether developmental costs are included and, if included, the period of time over which such costs are distributed; the rate of implementation; the concepts, skill, and ingenuity of the designers; and other factors. In the long run, lower costs with enhancement in levels of performance should be anticipated. Very large, short-term enhancements in system performance are likely to increase costs.

The phrase "library data processing" covers a broad spectrum of functions, processes, and varieties of data. Individual, current data bases may range from a few hundred thousand alphanumeric characters—for example, a library's outstanding order or "in-process" file—to more than 1 billion characters if the unique content of the public card catalog in a large university library is to be machine stored.

The spectrum of functions related to machine-readable data may include conventional library operations, for example, the preparation of book purchase orders; the preparation of bibliographical tools related to the library's holdings, notably the public and other catalogs; the provision of reader access to discipline- or mission-oriented bibliographical systems; and, in some cases, the provision of access to numerical or other kinds of nonbibliographical data bases, for instance, the 1970 census data.

Several observations may be made about this rather complex data environment. (1) Bibliographical and library operational data are intricately interrelated.[26] (2) Many of the bibliographical data bases contain data that to some degree may overlap with data in another system. (3) There is a strong movement to generate all, or at least much, of the basic bibliographical data for current publications outside of the academic library. (4) An increasingly

---

[26]The intricate relationships among many different kinds of data, from different sources, that are needed to fulfill a wide range of library operational and service functions may be illustrated by the data for a circulation system that may include: (1) name, address, borrower category, borrower number, etc. of all eligible borrowers; (2) bibliographical information sufficient to identify the material loaned, or to be loaned, by call number, author, title, date, ISBN, etc.; (3) information on the status of the loan, e.g., when made, when due, whether recalled for others, etc.; and (4) management data on loads and the responsiveness of the library to requests.

high percentage of the bibliographical data for current monographic publications and for some serial abstracting or indexing services is available to interested libraries in machine-readable form as well as in various printed forms. (5) There is the possibility of a substantial conversion into machine-readable form of the bibliographical data for current and retrospective serial titles and for noncurrent monographic material held by the Library of Congress and possibly other major scholarly libraries.[27]

These developments potentially offer the prospect of (1) making computer data processing for the library increasingly attractive, both as a service to readers and as a means of improving operations, and (2) providing an opportunity to shift away from a library-related bibliographical system that is heavily oriented to the holdings of a single institution to one based upon a national or an international literature base.

Existing or projected efforts to develop computer-based processing in academic libraries can be categorized or loosely grouped according to a number of characteristics. There are, for example, those applications where individual library processes or functions—for example, a serials holding list, a catalog card-set printing capability, a circulation-record system, a fiscal data system, a book-ordering system, etc.—have been the central focus, as contrasted with those applications in which an "integrated system" has been designed by means of which many different library functions or processes may be handled, utilizing parts or all of a more or less common data base. The first systems have been relatively easier and less costly to design, program, and operate. Designers have sometimes assumed that the transition from the first of these kinds of "systems" into a system of the second type would be feasible, but this may be more difficult than the planners anticipate. The second of these approaches offers a theoretical potential, depending upon the system design, of greater evolutionary capabilities and change. However, it should be noted that it is presently virtually impossible to specify in detail all current and future requirements in a very complex information-handling or large library environment. Thus the most prudent line of attack may be to build systems that can accommodate a broad range of discrete data elements concerned in one way or another with a bibliographic item, for example. This associated array of data can then be drawn upon to meet many different functional requirements.

A second set of design characteristics may relate to how the system's capabilities are expected to be used by, or to be related to, the ultimate user. Here there may be an extremely wide range of concepts, and some of the

---

[27]The prospects for retrospective conversion are presently not very bright because of the relatively high total cost. In the meantime many libraries are undertaking uncoordinated, nonstandard, and noncompatible local conversions. The aggregate costs of such record conversions will obviously be higher than a well-planned centralized effort, and results will be of relatively limited utility (see [4, 5, 18]).

literature suggests a rather sharp polarization between two different concepts of literature, information, and library access. The first concept is the use of computer-based data processing to generate essentially existing kinds of library products or services that are closely related to current library functions, for example, to generate printed card sets for card catalogs, to generate printed book catalogs, to print purchase orders, to search and to monitor outstanding order files, to assist in handling serial publications or to print lists of such publications, to handle circulation operations, etc.

The second concept sees the computer as providing an apparatus for a much more direct interaction with the user. Here the user, by means of a console and suitable instructions, may have a large file searched by computer in order to identify only that information or those documents that match the specified criteria; the user may conduct such a search from a point remote from the library or the computer; the results of the search may, at the user's discretion, be converted automatically into document requests, etc. These same techniques may be used by members of the library's staff for operational purposes.

There are inferences in a portion of the literature on library- and information-related data processing, that these are sharply divergent paths and that one must choose the "correct" path. Thus some of the advocates of real-time, interactive systems may seem to reject, as antiquated or unresponsive to users' needs, batch-produced catalogs, indices, or specialized bibliographies. It seems extremely important to recognize that the effective use of computer-based data processing does not, in itself, impose any mandatory pattern of access. To the contrary, the great long-term potential of computer-based data processing may well depend on the extraordinarily broad range of modes of access to a variety of data bases that it makes possible, as compared with existing manual processes. It will permit, at one end of the range, highly interactive search techniques and sophisticated data displays, and the search results can be coupled directly to systems of textual or document retrieval. Computer-based data processing will permit, at the other extreme, the fast generation of rather conventional-looking products. In between there are great possibilities for specialized printed indices or other tools that may be extremely useful.

The criteria for choosing the scope and nature of the data bases to be used, and the modes of access to such data bases, need to take into account a complex array of factors: for example, costs; user-related values associated with speed and mode of access; disciplinary as well as user variations in vocabularies, literature, and informational requirements; the quality and scope of the available data bases; the effect of loads; the state of the art for search strategies; the technical means of data storage, display, printout; and man-machine relationships; etc. It would be desirable to devise, for some period of time, information- or literature-access systems that permit a variety of modes of access and to observe with some care those approaches that seem most effective in particular circumstances and to ascertain the related cost differentials.

At least four generalizations seem relatively safe on the basic issues of access to computer-oriented data bases: (1) computer-based data processing, unlike most of the existing manual processes for bibliographical data, makes it technically and economically feasible to provide for a very wide range of modes of access to complex data bases; (2) the technologies and the costs of such access are likely to change and improve with time; (3) there may be a very wide range of user requirements in relation to modes of access and the scope of the data bases to be used; and (4) the cost/effectiveness ratios of alternative modes of access will require critical attention.

The spectrum of existing applications of computer data processing in library-related systems has included: book-fund fiscal accounting data; the generation of acquisition lists, specialized bibliographies, book catalogs, sets of catalog cards, sets of circulation charge cards, book-pocket labels, book-spine labels, lists of serial publications; serial check-in or issue-claiming processes; the selective dissemination to individuals of subject-profile-related bibliographical notices; catalog data editing and preparation; and a wide range of book circulation operations. There are a few library systems that permit either batch or on-line searching of a bibliographic data base for items that match designated search codes or specifications.

A number of computer-based mission-oriented or discipline-oriented literature-access systems have been created with capabilities for generating printed indices and abstracts and processing custom-specified searches of the data bases. Some of these systems, for example, the National Library of Medicine system (MEDLARS), have also been associated with a variety of means of access to the cited documents, that is, by photocopy, loan, or microfiche. Some of these data bases (there are now a great many) are used for the selective dissemination of information, despite the relatively high costs of such services. MEDLINE, operated through the National Library of Medicine and using a portion of the MEDLARS data base, is an example of a nationally available, on-line, literature-search system.

A number of major (and no doubt a larger number of minor) library-oriented systems have been announced but never developed, have been abandoned after partial development, or have been substantially cut back in design expectations after partial development. Some of the largest systems that have been abandoned have been in the hands of highly experienced, extremely large organizations, and the "failures" have represented, in a few cases, very substantial funds. Less conspicuous failures have probably been more common and less costly.

The major reasons for "failures" or significant reductions from planned or announced capability seem to be primarily due to the following factors: (1)

there have been failures to set operational and functional specifications realistically—a very difficult and complex task; (2) software design, development and maintenance difficulties have been substantially greater than anticipated, and consequently development costs have been much higher than anticipated; (3) shared computer operating costs have often been higher than anticipated; (4) the state of general computer operating systems has often left much to be desired in term of machine efficiency; (5) computers from different manufacturers have not been able to use the same software; (6) new generations of computers with new operating systems have not been able to handle programs designed to run on older operating systems and hardware; (7) computer storage capacity and input/output devices have caused difficulties or limitations; (8) efforts to place new systems into full operation have been made before the systems were adequately tested and debugged in full-scale operations; (9) there have been some serious intellectual-technical problems that are still not entirely solved—for example, the design of efficient systems for the management of very large files; (10) the library has been handicapped by the absence of cost data on existing services and the nearly complete absence of data relating to the values of improved information access; and (11) the availability of well-qualified, experienced personnel with all the requisite skills to design and program new systems has been limited.

Despite these difficulties, there have been some important and possibly illuminating "successes." Computers, like any other technology, can be used wisely or stupidly. The evidence seems persuasive that existing manually based processes, especially in very large research-oriented libraries, are likely to be less and less responsive to users' needs and more and more expensive. By contrast, it seems evident that computers can handle some kinds of library data in a functionally and cost-effective manner. The prospects for enhanced performance and lower unit costs are real, not illusory. The computer can also make possible new services that could not be achieved or economically justified with manually based systems, and can generate system performance or analytical data of great importance that simply cannot be captured with the present manual systems of operation.

CONCLUSIONS

How can the computer's capability best be utilized? In a sense there are a series of interrelated problems. The means of going from the existing pattern of largely locally oriented, library-bibliographical systems to the most highly cost-effective mode of computer application and utilization is *not* yet entirely obvious. Critical factors that will enable the technology to be used more easily are (1) the establishment of a format and coding standard (now rapidly becoming an international standard) for handling monographic and serial bibliographic data (see [4, 18]); and (2) the centralized output and general availability of large amounts of current and retrospective bibliographical data in machine-readable form under this standard. There are also an increasing number of serial abstracting and indexing tools which are based upon machine-readable data bases. These data bases, unfortunately, are *not* standardized, and standardization is moving very slowly indeed in this area. Costs of access to such data bases in many instances are substantial.[28]

Prior to the effective development of a new literature, information, or bibliographical system, there must be a careful specification of the functional requirements to be met. This set of issues has not always had the attention it requires. It is more difficult and complex than is commonly assumed. Second, one must find the means of designing and developing a capability that can efficiently respond to the specified functions.

The literature has tended to suggest two basic models in terms of functional requirements: (1) the first model proposes to respond to existing processes or functions of the library substantially as these functions now exist; (2) a second model in the literature is a technological kind of library, or alternative to the library, in which there will be instant access, from any point, for any user, to all information or recorded knowledge, at essentially zero or negligible cost. The first model seems, in many respects, a reasonable one from which to start if one is at the same time building a system that has a visibly strong capability for change and evolution. Without such a capability, large investments in system developments may soon prove to be too rigid and inflexible to meet changing functional needs and to exploit fully the relevant technologies. The second model is not presently feasible.

The wise and extensive use of computers and other suitable technologies, the availability of centrally as well as locally produced bibliographical data in machine-readable form, the clear recognition of users' needs, and the effect of economic pressures will all combine to change the library sufficiently to bring into serious question many existing library functions and processes. The research library of ten or fifteen years hence probably will not, in important respects, resemble either the current library model or the second model above. Nor will it be without books in large numbers. Among the changes already outlined are the following: (1) major alterations and improvements in the level of analysis, scope, and accessibility of the bibliographical apparatus (see [18]); (2) substantial reductions in the dependence upon repetitive clerical labor; (3) shared systems of efficient access to infrequently used research materials; and (4) significant improvements in the systems through which users may request and receive wanted materials.

Where the bibliographical apparatus is presently unsatisfactory, and where the costs can be met, there are certainly the prospect and capability of more complex and greatly improved search and retrieval operations. For

---

[28]For example, the *Newsletter* of the American Council of Learned Societies (January 1971) stated that the costs of the current tapes to an academic institution for the *Chemical Abstracts* services were $17,000 a year.

both users and library staff, where the costs and the service can be justified, there will surely be on-line access to processing, bibliographical, and circulation data; but the modes of such access, the size and nature of the data bases, and the means of querying such data bases seem less clear. That is, the costs and functional needs may not lead directly to cathode ray tube–keyboard, interactive, terminal systems for all bibliographical data bases for *all* kinds of uses. There is an essential need for the careful specification of requirements and the analysis of the costs and performance of a suitable range of alternative approaches. In such analysis and planning one must design any major new technologically based library system with genuine evolutionary capabilities. Such an approach may be more likely to succeed functionally and economically than systems planned to offer immediate but rather static benefits, unless these benefits are very large.

The general pattern of computer access for academic libraries has been that of sharing a university general-purpose computer. There are a few instances where the library (e.g., University of Toronto) has installed its own computer. In theory, library computer applications nicely complement other university computer uses. The library has high input-output requirements, very large storage requirements, and relatively low demands for core memory, at least for batch processing. Some of the current designs of more sophisticated systems for on-line access will require relatively large amounts of dedicated core, but there may be a design alternative here that could reduce this difficulty. A few academic libraries have tried to persuade computation-center staffs to design and develop "library systems" with the costs for machine and staff time to be carried by the computation center. In general, hard cash has worked better.

It is clear that as library functional requirements become larger in load size and more complex, the economic feasibility of a dedicated computer may become greater. So may the feasibility of one or more minicomputers coupled to a large central facility. The question of coupling library-oriented systems to a dedicated regional library-oriented computer; to a regional, national, or other educational computer network; or to a commercial computer utility will need to be assessed. The answer should be resolved by cost and technical considerations after one or more prototype systems are in operation and critically examined.

There has been some criticism that none of the existing, computer-based library data-processing systems was "transferable" from one institution to another as a package. That criticism reflects some misunderstanding of the functional design problems and the state of the computer art in terms of the general transferability of complex and reasonably efficient computer software packages. Obviously every university and college library cannot develop its own complex system. There are at least one or two prototype systems now under development that may offer substantial potentials for transferability.[29] Transfers in most cases will still require some degree of compatability in computer hardware (see [59]), the computer operating system, and input-output devices. Transfers will also require a substantial consensus on performance or functional requirements. Regional library-dedicated systems, such as that provided by the Ohio College Library Center, avoid the transfer problem but require some uniformity in patterns of use.

The long-term potential importance of computer-driven, high-speed, photoelectronic composition devices and computer output microform (COM) has already been noted. These technologies may be extremely valuable for the preparation and updating of printed bibliographies and catalogs at reasonable costs. They may also be very helpful in meeting the broad character font needs that are not well met by the speed or character sets available with conventional impact computer printers. There will still be input coding and other restraints for such large character sets as are required for Japanese and Chinese.

Libraries, like universities, tend to have very inadequate analytical data on their own operations and performance. Such data, especially as they relate to costs and system responses to user needs, are critically important in any effort to improve a library's efficiency and responsiveness; in the design of new services; in the identification and reduction of operating failures; in the analysis of costs and the effective planning of resource allocation; in the measurement of operating trends, work loads, and arrearages; in the formulation of operating policies; and in many other aspects of management. One of the most significant potentials of computer-based data processing relates to the opportunity to build into such systems efficient monitoring of many aspects of the library's performance.

---

[29] The University of Chicago Library Systems staff has been engaged in the design and development of a computer-based library data management system that, if found feasible, might greatly assist transferability by means of a software system that would, in a sense, decouple (1) input/output devices, (2) application software, (3) the computer operating system and computer, and (4) the data bases. A number of commercial, general-purpose data management systems are available, but they tend to require large amounts of core and are relatively inefficient in multiprocessing modes. Should the Chicago effort be successful, it could ease the transferability problem as well as make application programming easier (see Chapter 6).

6

EXAMPLES OF COMPUTER APPLICATIONS IN LIBRARY OPERATIONS AND INFORMATION ACCESS

In this chapter, there are descriptions of a very few, illustrative efforts to apply computer data processing, sometimes coupled with other technologies, primarily to academic library operations and to closely related information-access systems. The descriptive literature on such applications is very large (see [10, 17]), yet not very satisfactory: it is sometimes difficult to distinguish plans from achievements; many systems are still in an evolutionary state; detailed descriptions of capabilities are not generally available; and cost data are essentially absent. It has seemed inappropriate in this survey to try to make evaluative judgments on these applications because substantially more evidence than is available would be required in order to do so. There are, however, inferential, qualitative criteria that any observer may apply that relate primarily to the proposed levels of change in performance and the benefits or losses that may result from such change. There are a few indications of developmental and operating costs or estimates of costs in relation to prior systems or alternative solutions.

COLUMBIA UNIVERSITY[30]

The systems group at the Columbia University Libraries approached the use of data processing through the development of major subsystems as a means of planning and implementing an evolutionary development of an integrated system for handling library and bibliographical data. It was planned that the subsystems, where appropriate, would be combined to create a single integrated processing flow. Subsystems have been developed for computer processing of reserve book data and general circulation data; for two different, specialized data centers; for some acquisition and cataloging functions; for a union list of serials; and for some book-form catalogs. The approach to all of these systems has been batch-mode output. Columbia reports that the development and operating costs of these and other capabilities came to $1,105,000 over a five-year period (1966-70), including 40 percent fringe and overhead costs on salaries. The funding was principally from the National Science Foundation and Columbia University.

---

[30]The description of this project is based primarily upon the data in Fasana and Veaner [22, pp. 11-41].

COMPUTER APPLICATIONS

THE NATIONAL LIBRARY OF MEDICINE SYSTEM[31]

The National Library of Medicine has served as a national informational resource for the medical profession, although it was not officially called a National Library until 1956.

The Library has legislative authority for the following functions:
> (1) acquire and preserve books, periodicals, prints, films, recordings and other library materials pertinent to medicine; (2) organize the materials specified in clause (1) by appropriate cataloging, indexing, and bibliographical listings; (3) publish and make available the catalogs, indexes and bibliographies referred to in clause (2); (4) make available, through loans, photographic or other copying procedures, or otherwise, such materials in the Library as ... appropriate; (5) provide reference and research assistance; (6) engage in such other activities ... as [may be] appropriate and the Library's resources permit. [55]

1. *Monographic literature.*—The Library has published an index or catalog to its book collections from as early as 1880 (*Index Catalog of the Surgeon-General's Office*) with changes in name through the years, for example, 1950, *Armed Forces Medical Library Catalog*: 1966, *National Library of Medicine Current Catalog*. The last-mentioned publication lists current accessions.

2. *Journal literature.*—The National Library of Medicine receives approximately 23,000 current serial titles. Of these it processes for content approximately 6,000 currently active, substantive, journal titles from most countries of the world. It provides intellectual access to the contents of some 2,400 of these journals through the computer-based MEDLARS system (Medical Literature Analysis and Retrieval System). Articles are indexed by trained indexers in a number of locations in the United States and, under contract, in a number of foreign countries.

The MEDLARS system performs three major functions. (1) It provides rapid publication of the printed *Index Medicus*. (2) It can produce demand-search bibliographies. (3) It can produce recurring bibliographies, issued periodically on major subject areas and distributed by nonprofit organizations and federal agencies.

The MEDLARS demand-search system is now moving away from a batch-processing system to an on-line system. The on-line system, called MEDLINE (MEDLARS On-Line), is an extension of the AIM-TWX (Abridged Index Medicus-TWX) experimental on-line system which was initiated by the National Library of Medicine in May 1970. By July 1972 its data base included 450,000 citations from 1,200 of the leading journals indexed in *Index Medicus*—

---

[31]Mrs. Julie Virgo of the University of Chicago Graduate Library School faculty prepared the basic material upon which this summary statement has been based.

almost 60 percent of the citations printed in *Index Medicus* during the past three years. In February 1972 a communications network became operational, providing toll-free telephone access in about thirty-five cities to the MEDLINE data base at the National Library of Medicine. By the end of 1973, about 140 institutions are expected to be active MEDLINE users, and they will cover the related line and terminal costs.

3. *Interlibrary loan.*—The National Library of Medicine will provide, preferably through a local Regional Medical Library, loans or photocopies of journal articles not available locally.[32] Original volumes are loaned to U.S. libraries where extract photocopying is inappropriate. The Library provides TWX facilities.

4. *Regional Medical Library Program.*—In 1965, with the passage of the Medical Library Assistance Act, impetus was given to the planning of a national network to cover the information needs of the biomedical community. Ten major medical libraries have been designated as Regional Medical Libraries, and have been given partial federal support to serve a specific geographic area of the country. Within each region of several states, the smaller community hospital and medical society libraries rely on aid from the larger hospital and medical school library facilities. These libraries are backed up by the regional library, which, in turn, looks to the National Library of Medicine as the ultimate source of assistance or loan of material.

The interlibrary loan and photocopy services provided by the regional libraries have been supported by contracts with the National Library of Medicine. Each regional library also offers guidance and information services to its constituent libraries. All maintain direct communication with the National Library of Medicine by means of telephone and TWX.

All regional libraries and MEDLARS Centers (the two are usually, but not always, combined) have access to the MEDLINE system. As the MEDLINE capabilities develop, MEDLARS Centers will be phased out and replaced by MEDLINE Centers, providing services on the same basis as any other MEDLINE institution.

At the present time the program of the National Library of Medicine offers one of the most highly integrated and comprehensive information- and literature-access systems for a large group of users and a large body of literature.

NORTHWESTERN UNIVERSITY LIBRARY[33]

Northwestern University Library has in operation an on-line, data-pro-

---

[32]A suit for copyright infringement [56] has been filed against the United States by Williams and Wilkins, a publisher of several biomedical journals, in connection with this photocopy service. A hearing examiner for the U.S. Court of Claims has found for the plaintiff, the case has been argued before the Court, but a Court decision was still pending as this was written.

[33]This description is based upon an original statement prepared by the author which was subsequently reviewed and edited by John McGowan, April 26, 1972.

cessing system for both circulation and technical services. Book charges are processed on a self-service basis by the borrower using (1) a machine-readable book card, (2) a machine-readable I.D. card, and (3) any one of a series of remote, card-reading terminals that register the charge and produce a charge slip that the borrower places in the book. Books, upon return, are discharged by means of the machine-readable book card. Inquiry into the circulation file is by means of a typewriter terminal. The technical services system includes pre- and post-order searching and transfer of MARC data, purchase order preparation, on-line check-in of monographs and serials, catalog worksheet production, and catalog card production. On-line file update and inquiry is performed on typewriter terminals. Costs for development and operation are not available. Developmental funding was provided primarily through a special university fund. Costs for computer operations are apportioned between the line budgets of Circulation Services and Technical Services.

THE OHIO COLLEGE LIBRARY CENTER (OCLC)[34]

The OCLC presently offers to some fifty Ohio colleges and universities and a number of out-of-state institutions an on-line, interactive cataloging capability, and on-line access to a large union catalog of those holdings of member institutions that have been entered into the system's data base. Ultimately some five on-line, computer-access systems (with remote CRT [cathode ray tube]-keyboard consoles) have been proposed: (1) the presently available shared-cataloging data-access system, (2) a serials control system, (3) a user-remote catalog-access and circulation-control system, (4) other technical processing functions, and (5) user access to the data base by subject and title. A Xerox Data Systems Sigma 5 computer is presently in use with a specially developed operating system software package. In 1969-70 it was estimated that, with operation of the shared-cataloging capability, there would be Center costs of some $600,000 annually for systems operations, compared with costs for the related, superseded, manual procedures in the fifty-two member institutions estimated at $1 million, resulting in an aggregate theoretical savings of about $400,000. To achieve the projected savings, the participating libraries would need to reallocate $600,000 in salary savings for OCLC support. This reallocation, it has been acknowledged, may be difficult to achieve in all instances, since the OCLC system may not always entirely replace the need for functionally related local staff. However, Western College in Oxford, Ohio, reports net savings of $2,100 a year on a cataloging load of approximately 2,000 titles a year; Ohio University in Athens has reported substantial savings in cataloging costs, as has Dartmouth University.

---

[34]This description is based primarily on the OCLC *Annual Reports* for 1969-70, 1970-71, and 1971-72; the OCLC *Newsletter*; and letters and other information kindly supplied by Frederick G. Kilgour, February 15 and 23, 1972, and February 20 and April 20, 1973.

The present on-line efforts have been directed principally toward operation of the shared-cataloging concept, with the concurrent development of a major, on-line union catalog. By means of Library of Congress MARC II records and the records of any other library source that have been entered into the system, a cataloger at a remote location may, by means of a CRT-keyboard console, request the display of the pertinent cataloging data if available, enter additional data or alter existing data to meet any local requirements, or enter data for an entry not already in the file. The specified cataloging data are subsequently printed on cards at the Center in a batch mode and distributed by United Parcel Service. The system has provided, by means of several search keys, fast access to the large data files that are associated with the project. Records may presently be searched by the Library of Congress card number, by a title "key," or by an author-title "key." There are also LC card number and OCLC card number indexes.

The display of a bibliographic record also discloses the institutional holdings of members for material cataloged through the system. The on-line access to an up-to-date union catalog of the current and a portion of the retrospective holdings of the members can thus support, in addition to cataloging operations, interlibrary loan requests and, possibly, greater selectivity in purchases. As of February 1973, there were just over 560,000 bibliographical records in the data base. Expenditures for 1972–73 were budgeted at $842,322 (excluding grant funds for the support of research and development). Income was budgeted as follows: membership fees, $507,989; Ohio state grant, $193,333; catalog card income, $94,000; and other income, $47,000.

The Board of the Center has authorized extension of the system to other regions and out-of-state institutions.

THE OHIO STATE UNIVERSITY LIBRARIES' CIRCULATION SYSTEM[35]

Although a number of libraries have developed computer-based circulation systems, the Ohio State University Libraries have developed an on-line catalog-access and circulation system that has received substantial attention, in part because of the way in which the system is used. Library users may telephone requests to a central switchboard; items known to the reader are then keyed by library staff members on CRT-keyboard terminals, and entries matching the search key—constructed by letters taken from the name of the author and the title—are displayed showing the status of the item. If a copy is available, the user's identification number may also be keyed, a charge is recorded, and the book is subsequently paged and delivered.

The initial machine records for some 736,000 titles were keypunched at a unit cost of $0.128. The master file included 1,100,000 titles as of March 15,

---

[35]This description is based primarily on that in Cuadra [17, p. 196]; a letter from Gerry D. Guthrie, March 9, 1972; and a telephone conversation with Mr. Guthrie in March 1973.

1973. The initial cost per transaction was 13 percent higher (excluding development costs for the system and some computer personnel costs) than the prior manual costs. An IBM 370/155 computer is presently utilized for the system. Manual circulation costs were projected to increase at 5 percent per year on a unit basis, while the computer-based unit costs are expected to remain constant or to decline as the load increases. The circulation load has been growing at an annual rate of 15 percent, and unit cost savings over a manual system are projected during the third year of operation, exclusive of initial system development costs.

PROJECT INTREX, MASSACHUSETTS INSTITUTE OF TECHNOLOGY[36]

This large-scale project, the name of which is an acronym for information transfer experiments, was undertaken to create a foundation of experimental facts for the design of future large-scale information systems. The project has concentrated on (1) the assembly and organization of an information store of sufficient size in a selected field of science and technology, and (2) the development of the essential facilities for storing, retrieving, transmitting, and displaying that information. The underlying concept has involved (1) the generation of a more detailed subject analysis of a defined body of literature than is commonly available, (2) the machine storage of this analytical data, and (3) improved systems of textual access for the cited materials.

The INTREX data base can be searched from a number of remote locations by means of instructions presented on teletypewriter or CRT-keyboard terminals. If desired citations are found in such a search, the project offers a wide range of systems for remote, real-time, document/textual access via coaxial cables, including CRT display, or the production at some terminals of a microform copy, from which a full-size copy can be made by the user on ancillary equipment. A variety of specialized hardware has been developed for the system. The general objective is to provide to a remote reader the capability of a custom search of a document-related data base that may more accurately establish the existence and relevance of a body of literature, and to provide access to that literature without delay and without impairing any other user's access. As of 1972 the INTREX "file" consisted of more than 17,000 documents from recent technical literature. The system thus far has cost approximately $3,600,000 to develop. The director of the project had hoped to extend the literature base, between 1972 and 1975, to 1 million items and to offer a regional service to 5,000 physicists and electrical engineers in New England. This three-year extension would cost an estimated additional $2,341,000. On the basis of studies by Dr. C. W. Therrien of Project INTREX, Dr. Overhage has estimated the costs for operating the

---

[36]This description of the INTREX project is based primarily upon the following: Carl F. J. Overhage, *Project INTREX: A Brief Description* (Cambridge, Mass.: M.I.T. Press, 1971); and letters from Dr. Carl F. J. Overhage, February 17 and October 2, 1972.

proposed expanded system, once established, at around $900,000 annually, or at an estimated cost of around $120–$240 annually per user. It was understood, as of early 1973, that such funding had not been secured and that Project INTREX would be terminated. The possible effect of copyright restrictions on the textual-access segment of systems of this kind could be adverse.

STANFORD UNIVERSITY[37]

The Stanford University Library, in collaboration with the Stanford University Computation Center and the Institute for Communication Research, has been engaged for more than six years in "developing a system that would allow us to take advantage of the most advanced computer technology ... available, namely, third generation equipment with its on-line access to files through visual terminals. Our original intent was to support only file oriented functions, such as technical processing and circulation, and to stay away from reference or information retrieval." In 1968 two Stanford projects (SPIRES [Stanford Public Information Retrieval System] and BALLOTS [Bibliographic Automation of Large Library Operations using a Time Sharing system]) were merged "with the goal of creating common software usable for both library automation and information retrieval."

Funding was originally from the U.S. Office of Education ($1,200,000) and the National Science Foundation ($1,130,000) and currently is from the Council on Library Resources and the National Endowment for the Humanities ($650,000). The past developmental cost for the BALLOTS project (primarily library related) was estimated to be $1,407,600, and future developmental costs were estimated in September 1971 to be $2,170,000. The first module was operational in autumn 1972. The annual operating costs have been estimated at $400,000–$450,000, of which approximately 75 percent would be for computer operating costs and hardware. The SPIRES system is operated as a subprocessor under the general computer operating system. It is thus available to any one using the Computation Center, and current use costs are recovered as user charges. The BALLOTS system relies on more than one-half of the SPIRES software for its general file handling services. The developmental, as distinguished from the operating, costs of SPIRES are not included in the developmental costs listed.

The overall system is projected to maintain in an on-line mode of access "very large data files containing Library of Congress data and Stanford in-process and final cataloging data." The on-line terminals projected for the system for inquiries would require about 40 percent of the costs of system operation. No net savings from the system are projected for the "next decade." The justification for the system is the expected added convenience

---

[37]The description of this project is based primarily upon Fasana and Veaner [22, pp. 42–68], Weber [58], and a letter from David Weber, February 22, 1973.

and savings in time for the students, staff, and faculty in ascertaining whether the library holds desired material and whether it is available, and in handling requests for it. "Other justifications are the slowing of escalating personnel costs, the elimination of monotonous routines, greater record accuracy, and the beginning of an increasingly useful data base for local and interlibrary management."

THE UNIVERSITY OF CHICAGO LIBRARY[38]

The University of Chicago library systems project has been engaged since 1966 in the development of a computer-based bibliographic data-processing system for a large university library. The total program of development is best described in two phases.

The first phase, 1966-70, was for the development of a basic bibliographic data-processing system designed to handle record generation, processing, and record maintenance for library technical processing operations. The system design emphasized printed products such as catalog cards, purchase orders, charge cards, selection lists, and processing slips.

A basic requirement was for the system to handle all aspects of bibliographic data processing. Because of this a major developmental effort necessarily went into the analysis, definition, and design required to handle the enormous detail of bibliographic and other library data by machine. Standard computer capabilities were used in the development, including hardware, operating system software, and programming languages. The resulting system is quite versatile in handling bibliographic data and records: data can be entered into the system or from MARC tapes, records can be created and updated as needed for any process, and output from these records can be scheduled at any time, formatted and arrayed in ways most appropriate to their use.

To sum up, the first-phase development required an intensive and frequently pioneering analytical and design effort to define library and bibliographic detail and to implement highly original systems using standard computer equipment and operating software. A large-scale data-processing operation that emphasizes printed products has resulted. The system has been in day-to-day operation on one of the University Computation Center's computers (successively, an IBM number 360/30, 360/40, 360/50, and 360/65 since 1968; a shift to an IBM 370/168 is expected in 1973). By the end of 1972, some 2 million individually formatted catalog cards for the library's catalogs had been produced by this system, along with many other products.

A by-product of the operation has been the build up of a large data base of machine-readable bibliographic records. The major limitation of the first-phase system has been the lack of effective on-demand access to selected

---

[38]This description is based essentially on a summary statement prepared by Charles T. Payne, head of Systems Development in the University of Chicago Library.

items in this data base. There has been a continuing absence in the field of adequate generalized file-management software that could economically provide multiple points of access for a large, library-oriented data base. This affected development during the first-phase and led to a shift in emphasis for the second stage.

In the second phase the development of a Library Data Management System to provide the needed basic software capabilties was proposed, rather than further construction of a new system or modules with inadequate file-handling capabilities.

The first task of this second stage was to design and put into operation a computer system with highly generalized capabilities for handling library data and files. Library data elements have many complex and subtle relationships that must be explicitly recognized and handled by an effective system. Library files are very large, complex, and difficult to manage economically. Data management requirements include handling multiple large and complex on-line files, indexing them, and providing access to the data.

The Library Data Management System design actually consists of several functionally related software packages. One package is a data-base (file) management system. This system provides maintenance of the data bases according to prior definitions, provides logical access to data from programs, and provides integrity and security in the data bases. An access control module provides, among other things, control of the different access and indexing methods required, that is, inverted-file and direct-access methods. An on-line control system provides the interface between external input-output devices and the applications programs and between these programs and the files (via the data-base management system). The on-line control system handles all device-dependent software, message collection and routing, program scheduling and intercommunication, etc.

Library application programs are another package. These programs will perform certain specific library functions such as bibliographical searching, acquisitions, and circulation routines. Designing and building these programs is the second major task of this developmental phase.

It is the view of the University of Chicago Library Systems staff that the overall design of this system accomplishes a number of important objectives by providing rather clear software compartments between (1) the data-base management system, (2) the handling of input-output data and external devices, (3) the application programs, (4) the data base, and (5) the computer operating system. Benefits of this include simpler application programming, program testing, and maintenance; greater versatility in the development of applications; better capability for subsequent change and evolution of the system; greater freedom from hardware restraints; and high operational efficiency. The system is expected to have a relatively high potential for institutional transfer or the shared use of the system either by a number of users within an institution or by a number of institutions. At the University of Chicago the Library Data Management System capabilities will also be utilized by other Computation Center users with large-file processing applications.

Developmental support in the amount of $602,000 for the first phase was given by the National Science Foundation over a four-and-a-half-year period, plus substantial university support. The second phase is being funded by the university and by a joint grant from the National Endowment for the Humanities and the Council on Library Resources amounting to $800,000 over a four-year period. The purchase costs for a substantial number of terminals and a mini-computer to interface with the university's main computer are being funded by a grant of $350,000 from the Joseph and Helen Regenstein Foundation.

The technical processing system and the on-line circulation system are expected to be in full operation by late 1974. The staff, in a detailed study of economic feasibility, has projected net operating cost savings of increasing amounts beginning in 1975-76. The projected savings allow for an eight-year rate of amortization for terminal and mini-computer purchase costs, but do not include the system design and developmental costs. The systems staff believes the system will be highly responsive to many different patterns of large-file use.

CONCLUSION

There are, of course, many other computer-based library bibliographical or operational systems as well as many information systems, some of which are coupled to microform text access, printed bibliographies or indexes, abstracts, and selective dissemination or other information services. Those so briefly described above are only to suggest something of the range of current efforts. Many of these and other systems are described in the *Annual Review of Information Science and Technology* [17] and other references previously cited.

In an essentially new field there is likely to be some strength—funds permitting—related to reasonable divergence in problem definition and the methods of attack. Such differences in approach offer some protection against the inevitable failures and, more important, present an opportunity for the evaluation of alternative approaches or solutions. However, a situation may be developing in which many libraries are attempting, and in some cases being pressed, to choose this or that course of action with repect to the adoption of machine-based bibliographical access and processing, where processes for the independent evaluation of capabilities are weak. Relevant criteria and objective evidence for making such choices or evaluations, with a high degree of assurance that the choices will be sound over the reasonably distant future, are not presently readily available. The problem is one of substantial inherent difficulty. Given an environment in which there may be momentum "to automate now," this is a situation involving considerable risk.

The economic and intellectual feasibility of library or bibliographical data processing will be very directly affected by the one-time generation of, and access to, suitable bibliographical data of high quality. In this connection it is extremely important to recognize the critical role of the Library of Congress. The establishment of an internationally accepted standard format for handling machine-readable bibliographical data; the preparation and distribution of substantial amounts of such data for current publications in English;[39] the exploration of the means and recognition of the strong desirability of converting retrospective bibliographical data on a central, systematic, high-quality basis; and a variety of related matters have been among the Library of Congress' major contributions to this field. These efforts have been clearly summarized by Henriette Avram and others [4, 5]. It is hoped by many that the Library of Congress will seek the necessary appropriations to pursue these matters even more vigorously. The long-term national benefits would be very substantial.

---

[39]Publications in French are to be added in 1974.

7

SOME GENERAL OBSERVATIONS AND CONCLUSIONS

The preceding chapters have offered a number of conclusions and observations related to the general topics of each chapter. In this final chapter an effort is made to restate a number of these observations and to add a few other points in a more general context.

This report has been limited essentially to the problems of literature and information access in the academic sector at the level of graduate studies and research. There are, of course, substantial overlapping uses and shared concerns with the problems of the undergraduate library; the small and large public library; the special library; societies and private organizations engaged in publishing, bibliographic, or other information-related activities; state library agencies; and many branches of the federal government. The effort to concentrate on the problems at the level of graduate study and research is justified by the conviction that it is here that the library problems are intrinsically most difficult, and by the view that if more effective responses can be found in these areas, there will be benefits to many other fields, while the reverse effect is less likely. It must be recognized that the library, information, and literature needs of users at the level of advanced research and graduate study display an extraordinary range of critically important differences. An assumption that the informational and literature needs of the clinical investigator and those of the historian of sixteenth-century France are similar in their basic characteristics, and differ only in subject matter, can lead only to trouble. It is all too easy to blur or otherwise fail to recognize these differences.

The major contemporary issues in the field of information and literature access emerge from and are affected by a number of interesting forces or circumstances. (1) There is substantial evidence that many readers and sectors of society are seeking, or are in need of, more efficient and assured access to pertinent data or literature than is presently available. (2) There is a strong presumption, but little supporting evidence, that improved access to information and literature would be of either immediate or long-term benefit to society, and that a failure to enhance such systems of access where possible may carry high, but unspecified, penalties or costs. (3) There is abundant evidence that there are presently available a variety of technologies and other, equally important measures that, if wisely used, could significantly enhance information- and literature-access systems. (4) It is fairly evident that systems of access to information and literature are essentially open-ended in terms of many basic characteristics such as scope, quality, user convenience, speed and assurance of access, degree of synthesis, currency, etc. (5) There is also rather clear evidence of current fiscal trends, literature growth, and inflexibilities in current library and other tools, systems, or practices that, unless altered, will result in further deterioration in the related cost/effectiveness ratios.

Effective, long-term responses to these and related problems will require a variety of rather basic changes in research library concepts and operations. The changes must be focused on improving the cost/effectiveness ratios of three major aspects of the library: (1) the bibliographical apparatus through which pertinent literature and information are identified and located, (2) the accessibility of the literature resource and information base, and (3) library processing functions and other aspects of library service and operations.

It is the bibliographical apparatus, frequently coupled with local library processing or status data, that enables a student or scholar to learn (1) whether literature or information exists that seems relevant to a particular need; (2) the probable degree of relevance of the identified material or data; (3) whether the material is locally available and, if so, where it has been placed and its current availability status; and (4) if it is not locally available, the probabilities and means of obtaining it from some other source. While many uses of a good library successfully bypass some of these steps, the serious user is likely to encounter many of these problems with some frequency. The margin for error, frustration, uncertainty, or failure is clearly very great.

The primary objective in connection with the bibliographical apparatus should be to design, develop, and evaluate a broad range of bibliographical tools and other access mechanisms centered, at least initially, primarily on the monographic literature. The initial data for such tools should come from the LC MARC II data base, augmented as rapidly as possible by as much of the current LC-NPAC (National Program for Acquisitions and Cataloging) data as existing computer character set capability will permit. As soon thereafter as possible, the Library of Congress should seek funding for the large-scale conversion to digital form of its own, and other high-quality, standard retrospective bibliographical data. The bibliographical tools or indexes should be designed for different user groups or institutional needs with a wide range of approaches and modes of access, for example, author, title, permuted titles, subject, subject classification, geographic origin, date of publication, and language. This information should be available in printed form, COM form, and by means of batch or on-line custom searching, depending upon needs, loads, and other circumstances.

Very careful attention should be given to the optimal modes and scope of such outputs, the most effective format for the printed outputs, the costs, and user utility and reactions. The printed outputs should be directed toward potential individual use as well as institutional usage. Cumulations may be based upon literature growth rates and patterns of use. The basic objectives of such a development should be (1) to enhance the means by which potential users may easily learn of the existence of pertinent materials, and (2) to reduce the costs and complexity of the local library bibliographical tools. The analogy for the development of such an approach is that of the well-designed discipline- or mission-oriented serial abstracting and indexing tools and capabilities.

The primary data bases could be partially or fully duplicated according to requirements to meet many other bibliographical as well as local or regional library processing requirements.

There are a number of implications of such a proposal. A primary bibliographical apparatus, no longer based upon the resources of a local library, theoretically should become more "portable" and accessible and thus reduce existing geographic or institutional inequalities in bibliographical access. The availability of such tools would be likely to augment the effective use of the cited literature.

Such an apparatus would make it nearly imperative that there be incorporated within the "generalized" bibliographical apparatus—whether library-generated or not—some devices that would make it much easier for the user to locate and secure desired items from either a local library or a suitable alternative source. It has been suggested in this report that one potential device to help meet this objective may be the ISBN (International Standard Book Number) and ISSN (International Standard Serial Number). The inclusion of these numbers in scholarly bibliographies, footnotes, and other sources could greatly simplify the task of locating those items that have such numbers. For those disciplines that rely heavily upon recent literature, the approach could be very helpful within a five- to ten-year period.

Clearly, there are many unstated problems of bibliographical systems design, organization, support, priority determination, implementation, and evaluation; but most of the essential elements to establish such a system are already visible. Such a system would, of course, be critically dependent upon computer data processing. The optimal organizational mechanism for a large-scale bibliographical output may be that of a not-for-profit or a government corporation which would rely upon federal funding as well as library and user charges.

There are several important generalizations about this or similar proposals, especially those relating to technology. The specifications for the "perfect" or "ultimate" information-literature-library-access system are not known. For this reason if for no others, the development of such information-literature–access systems should be incremental and evolutionary. Wise evolutionary development can tolerate some kinds of minor errors and permit carefully planned as well as some unplanned or opportunistic responses to unforeseen needs. The high rate of change in technological capabilities also argues for an evolutionary pattern of development. The absence of a recognized cost/benefit relationship may even require such a pattern to insure that the required support for each new level of capability can be secured and sustained. If these views are accepted, the questions are then essentially: In which direction do we plan the road, and how fast can we go (Licklider, in [9, pp. 310-11])?

The System Development Corporation [53] and others have noted the relative absence of strong organizational mechanisms to effect basic changes in library- and information-access systems. It is possible that the absence of suitable organizational structures may be a less difficult obstacle than concepts that may be too limiting or the possible absence of a consensus among librarians and users as to anticipated rates of changes, priorities, and desirable goals. There seems to be a substantial professional library consensus that sees technology as essentially aiding existing library resource development concepts and processes, but possibly with relatively little basic alteration in the library's fiscal resource allocations. There are also suggestions from technologists and others for the very large-scale, on-line, interactive, data- and textual-access systems that would, it is asserted, reallocate resources in such a way as to supersede the library in many or most of its traditional functions. The cited major studies strongly indicate that the first of these positions, if it exists, may not long be found tenable. The second is unlikely to be currently feasible except for very small bodies of data.

The second major area where new approaches seem desirable relates to document, textual, or information access. Some 60 percent of the expenditures of large libraries may be devoted to the purchase of books, serials, and other materials, the related binding, and the associated cataloging and other processing costs. This percentage of library expenditures is so high as to require critical attention in terms of the cost effectiveness of the function as it relates to the user, to the individual library, and to large numbers of such libraries examined in the aggregate. There are many reasons to believe that the most cost-effective solution to this problem is to establish one (or a very few) national pools for the acquisition of current serial and monographic resources on as comprehensive a basis as possible—duplicating, for example, LC-NPAC and PL-480 acquisition programs and adding current serials to that base. Such a facility would (1) extend the resource base of virtually every library in the country, (2) enable individual libraries to be more selective in local acquisitions where desired, (3) enable local libraries to duplicate to a greater degree materials for which there is high local demand, and (4) limit space and processing costs to materials of relatively high demand, or of relatively high quality, or of sustained institutional interest. Access to such pools would be through the loan of originals and photocopying where the latter is legally permissable and economically advantageous.

There is a professional library view that a superior alternative to the central "pool" concept for back-up resources would be based upon a division of acquisition responsibilities among existing libraries by designated subject fields or other categories and a reliance upon an improved system of interlibrary loan for access. This seems likely to be more costly in aggregate expenditures, less stable, less reliable, less comprehensive, and a slower system of access for contemporary and future acquisitions than a centralized-pool approach.

To improve the availability of retrospective materials—as distinguished from current and future publications—it is not economically feasible to duplicate for a central pool the present resources of the major research libraries. In consequence, access to such materials will need to be provided principally by improved systems of interlibrary loan and photocopying. Interlibrary loan systems require more equitable support as between lenders and borrowers, more efficient means of locating desired materials, a reduction of paper work, more equitable load distribution, and greater speed. Libraries have tried textual facsimile as a means of interlibrary resource utilization without encouraging results. The technology will need to improve in quality and decline in costs to be attractive.

The entire spectrum of microform and other photocopying technologies is relevant to (1) limited or on-demand publication of some materials, (2) interlibrary or "pool" resource access, and (3) assembling large collections of pertinent materials for on-demand loan or *en bloc* acquisition. The latter has been important in terms of access to retrospective resources and preservation. Microform technology is the center of considerable current interest, and there are a number of forecasts of increasing utilization. The handicaps in microform technology have been largely related to the relative difficulty in its use, the lack of sufficient standardization, and the absence of a complete, easily accessible, reliable, inexpensive system that would permit the user to go from full-size copy to microform, microform to microform, and microform to full-size copy. The recent introduction of very high-reduction microforms, the recent announcement of a new method for microform image formation, the continuing development of a wide range of full-size electrostatic copying techniques, COM technology, and recurring proposals for high-density storage or transmission of data by means of lasers, holography, video disks, or other technologies suggest that the potential impact of these technologies upon libraries and library services may increase significantly. The work of scholarship would be enhanced with an appropriate amendment to the existing copyright act that would suitably define the concept of fair use of copyrighted material in terms of photocopying.

Library resources exist primarily on wood-pulp paper, the life of which, under the usual conditions for storage and use, is quite limited. There are presently some encouraging prospects for the development of one or more large-scale systems for chemically treating such books and papers in ways that will greatly extend their useful lifetimes. Should such processes fail to materialize, very large-scale microform copying will probably be the only suitable alternative. For the future, there are also some encouraging developments with respect to the possibility of manufacturing highly durable papers that would be competitive in costs and printing quality with existing book papers.

The third area where the possibility of major changes in cost effectiveness were suggested is that of library processing and operating functions. The large library in its own operations and in relation to many services to users—for example, circulation control, catalog access—is a labor-intensive enterprise that is heavily dependent upon a very large and extremely complex set of data bases. These and other characteristics, associated with the well-known unit cost trends in repetitive manual tasks as compared with well-designed machine-based systems, argue for the utilization of the computer in library operations where it can be cost effective. Computer data processing also offers the prospect of providing enhanced performance and new kinds of service. The case for computer technology as an aid to library and bibliographical processes seems very strong, despite some serious and costly errors in the design and development of some computer-based library capabilities or information systems. Such failures are not uncommon in new applications of complex technologies, nor are they unknown in more traditional enterprises. Failures to employ a complex, difficult, and relevant technology wisely must be recognized essentially as conceptual, design, or implementation failures. The technology may not be at fault, only the way it was used.

Although the probability appears high that most large libraries will make increasing use, directly or indirectly, of computer-based data processing, the mechanisms and structures for such utilization are much less clear. It is assumed that a very high proportion of the diversified, general bibliographical output, especially those outputs in printed or COM form, would be most efficiently generated from a national center or not-for-profit agency. However, there will continue to be a need for local access to and use of bibliographical data. It is evident that the independent, local design and development of sophisticated library data-processing capabilities and bibliographic searching capabilities is not likely to be either feasible or necessary. Yet there is a need to provide for such capabilities. These needs could be met by "package" systems of various sizes and capabilities; by systems developed by special groups to meet their own special requirements—if there are such; by central systems serving a region; by systems effectively operated as national utilities; or by some pattern of hybrid capabilities and relationships. There is presently insufficient experience or well-demonstrated capability to make sound predictions in this matter. The long-run configuration is very likely to be some type of hybrid system with local systems of different sizes and capabilities interfacing with more general and larger capabilities and capacities.

In any case, there is, or there will very shortly be, a need for the careful and objective evaluation of emerging prototype data-processing capabilities. Such evaluations will have to consider overall system performance in relation to carefully specified current and projected objectives or requirements, loads and capacities, costs, operational and staff impact, evolutionary or adaptablility characteristics, system reliability, hardware restraints, etc.

It is unlikely that *large* increases in library response capabilities, services, or resources can be quickly and easily achieved at little or no incremental cost. However, over a reasonable period of time, with a well-conceived incremental development program, one may anticipate substantial improvements in capabilities and stable or even reduced unit service costs. The carrying through of such a development will require a suitable organizational structure, reduced institutional autonomy, a substantial scholarly and professional consensus on the objectives, and some wise and statesman-like planning and implementation.

Fiscal support for both development and operations may need to be shared among federal sources, library or academic budgets, philanthropic sources, and, in some instances, user charges for special services. The current prospects for federal as well as other sources of developmental and ongoing operational funding for enhanced services seem rather bleak. The prospects would surely be strengthened by sound plans for which there is widespread support. There has been a substantial momentum, under the stimulus of the Library Services and Construction Act, to channel federal funds for shared library enterprises into state-oriented systems. For the development of shared capabilities at the research level, either national or large regional approaches are likely to be much more effective and less costly. Other federal legislation exists that could support activities of the kind outlined if appropriations were to be made.

There can be little doubt that the large research library can and will change in relation to the needs of scholarship and other forces or circumstances. There are economic and other factors that can force some kinds of change whether planned or not. This being so, the pertinent questions become: Will the direction of prospective changes be favorable or unfavorable? What are the means through which favorable changes can best be achieved? What are the objectives and priorities? How rapidly can constructive changes be effected? The wise use of selected, currently available technologies, associated with a number of equally important nontechnological changes, now offers a major opportunity for improving the quality and scope of access to literature and information and the long-term cost effectiveness ratio of the library.

REFERENCES

1. Association of Research Libraries. *Academic Library Expenditures, 1971-72*. Washington, D.C.: Association of Research Libraries, 1972 (and prior years).
2. Association of Research Libraries. *Newsletter*, April 23, 1973, p. 8.
3. *Automation and the Library of Congress*. Survey sponsored by the Council on Library Resources, Inc., submitted by Gilbert W. King and others. Washington, D.C.: Library of Congress, 1963.
4. Avram, Henriette D. *RECON Pilot Project: Final Report on a Project Sponsored by the Library of Congress, the Council on Library Resources, Inc., and the U.S. Department of Health, Education, and Welfare, Office of Education*. Washington, D.C.: Library of Congress, 1972.
5. Avram, Henriette D.; Maruyama, Lenore S.; and Rather, John C. "Automation Activities in the Processing Department of the Library of Congress." *Library Resources and Technical Services* 16 (Spring 1972): 195-239.
6. Ballou, Hubbard W., ed. *Guide to Reproduction Equipment*. 5th ed. Silver Spring, Md.: National Microfilm Assn., 1971.
7. Baumol, W. J., et al. "The Costs of Library and Information Services." In *Libraries at Large*, edited by Douglas M. Knight and E. Shepley Nourse. New York: R. R. Bowker Co., 1969.
8. Baumol, William J., and Matityahn, Marcus. *Economics of Academic Libraries*. Washington, D.C.: American Council on Education, 1973.
9. Becker, Joseph, ed. *Conference on Interlibrary Communications and Information Networks*. Chicago: American Library Association, 1971.
10. Billingsley, Alice, comp. "Bibliography of Library Automation." *American Libraries* 3 (March 1972): 289-312.
11. Bowen, William G. *The Economics of the Major Private Universities*. Berkeley, Calif.: Carnegie Commission on Higher Education, 1968.
12. *The Bowker Annual of Library and Book Trade Information 1972*. New York: R. R. Bowker Co., 1972 (and prior years).
13. Buckle, D. G. R., and French, Thomas. "The Application of Microform to Manual and Machine-readable Catalogs." *Program: News of Computers in Libraries* 6 (July 1972): 187-203.
14. Carter, Launor F., et al. *National Document Handling Systems for Science and Technology*. Study undertaken for the Committee on Scientific and Technical Information (COSATI) by the System Development Corporation. New York: John Wiley & Sons, 1967.

REFERENCES

15. Clapp, Verner W. "The Copyright Dilemma: A Librarian's View." *Library Quarterly* 38 (October 1968): 352-87.
16. Conference Board. *Information Technology: Some Critical Implications for Decision Makers.* New York: Conference Board, Inc., 1972.
17. Cuadra, Carlos, ed. *Annual Review of Information Science and Technology.* Vol. 6. Chicago: Encyclopaedia Britannica, Inc., 1971.
18. DeGennaro, Richard. "A National Bibliographical Data Base in Machine Readable Form: Progress and Prospects." *Library Trends* 18 (April 1970): 537-50.
19. Dix, William S. "Financial Problems of University Libraries: A Summary." Mimeographed. [Princeton, N.J.]: Association of American Universities, March 1954.
20. Downs, Robert B., et al. *University Library Statistics.* Washington, D.C.: Association of Research Libraries, 1969.
21. Dunn, Oliver C., et al. *The Past and Likely Future of 58 Research Libraries, 1951-1980: A Statistical Study of Growth and Change.* West Lafayette, Ind.: Purdue University, May 1971.
22. Fasana, Paul J., and Veaner, Allen, eds., *Collaborative Library Systems Development.* Cambridge, Mass.: M.I.T. Press, 1971.
23. Fry, George, and Associates. *Survey of Copyrighted Material Reproduction Practices in Scientific and Technical Fields.* Chicago: George Fry & Associates, 1962.
24. Fussler, Herman H., and Simon, Julian L. *Patterns in the Use of Books in Large Research Libraries.* Chicago: University of Chicago Press, 1969.
25. Hays, David G. *A Billion Books for Education in America and the World: A Proposal.* Memorandum RM 5574-RC. Santa Monica, Calif.: Rand Corp., April 1968.
26. Henderson, Madeline M., comp. *Proceedings of the Conference on Image Storage and Transmission Systems for Libraries ... Dec. 1969, at the U.S. Bureau of Standards.* PB no. 193692. Springfield, Va.: Clearinghouse for Federal, Scientific, and Technical Information, 1970.
27. Hopp, Ralph H., comp. *ARL Academic Library Statistics.* Minneapolis: University of Minnesota Library, 1971.
28. Kaltwasser, Franz George. "The Quest for Universal Bibliographical Control." *Wilson Library Bulletin* 46 (June 1972): 895-901.
29. Kemeny, John G. *Man and the Computer.* New York: Charles Scribner's Sons, 1972.
30. Kilgour, Frederick G. "The Economic Goal of Library Automation." *College and Research Libraries* 30 (July 1969): 307-11.
31. Larkworthy, Graham, and Cyril G. Brown. "Library Catalogs on Microfilm." *Library Association Record* 73 (December 1971): 231-32.
32. Licklider, J. C. R. *Libraries of the Future.* Cambridge, Mass.: M.I.T. Press, 1965.

REFERENCES

33. Line, Maurice B.; Brittain, J. J.; and Crammer, F. A. *Investigation into Information Requirements of the Social Sciences.* Vol. 1, Text. Bath: Bath University Library, 1971.
34. Lipetz, Ben-Ami. "Catalog Use in a Large Research Library." *Library Quarterly* 46 (January 1972): 129-39.
35. Lipetz, Ben-Ami. *User Requirements in Identifying Works in a Large Library.* New Haven, Conn.: Yale University Library, June 1970.
36. Locke, William N. "Computer Costs for Large Libraries." *Datamation* 16 (February 1970): 69-74.
37. Mason, Ellsworth. "The Great Gas Bubble Prick't; or, Computers Revealed—by a Gentleman of Quality." *College and Research Libraries* 32 (May 1971): 183-88.
38. Millet, John D. *Financing Higher Education in the United States.* New York: Columbia University Press, 1952.
39. National Academy of Sciences. Committee on Scientific and Technical Communication. *Scientific and Technical Communication, Pressing National Problem and Recommendations for Its Solution.* Washington, D.C.: National Academy of Sciences, 1969.
40. National Academy of Sciences. Information Systems Panel. Computer Science and Engineering Board. *Libraries and Information Technology: A National System Challenge.* Report to the Council on Library Resources, Inc. Washington, D.C.: National Academy of Sciences, 1971.
41. National Research Council. Committee on Information in the Behavioral Sciences. *Communication Systems and Resources in the Behavioral Sciences.* Washington, D.C.: National Academy of Sciences, 1967.
42. National Research Council. Council on Biological Sciences Information. *Information Handling in the Life Sciences.* Washington, D.C.: National Research Council, February 1970.
43. Overhage, Carl F. J., and Harmon, Joyce R., eds. *INTREX: Report of a Planning Conference on Information Transfer Experiments.* Cambridge, Mass.: M.I.T. Press, 1965.
44. *Report of the Commission on the Humanities.* American Council of Learned Societies, Council of Graduate Schools in the United States, and United Chapters of Phi Beta Kappa. New York: American Council of Learned Societies, 1964.
45. Sharpe, John L., III, and Evans, Esther, eds. *The Dedication of the William R. Perkins Library: Proceedings.* April 15-16, 1970. Durham, N.C.: Duke University Library, 1971.
46. Shoffner, Ralph M. "Economics of National Automation of Libraries." *Library Trends* 18 (April 1970): 448-63.
47. Spigai, Frances G. *The Invisible Medium: The State of the Art of Microform and a Guide to the Literature.* Washington, D.C.: ERIC Clearinghouse on Library and Information Sciences, in cooperation with

REFERENCES

the ASIS Special Interest Group on Reprographic Technology, March 1973.

48. Stevens, Rolland E. *A Feasibility Study of Centralized and Regionalized Interlibrary Loan Centers.* Prepared for the Association of Research Libraries. Washington, D.C.: Association of Research Libraries, April 1973.

49. Stuart-Stubbs, Basil. *Developments in Library and Union Catalogues and the Use of Microform in British Libraries.* Report of an inquiry conducted on behalf of the Canadian Union Catalogue Task Group. Ottawa: National Library of Canada, Research and Planning Branch, March 1973.

50. Stuart-Stubbs, Basil. *Purchasing and Copying Practices at Canadian University Libraries: Two Studies Performed for the Canadian Association of College and University Libraries, Committee on Copyright Legislation.* Ottawa: Canadian Library Association, 1971.

51. Swanson, Don R. "Design Requirements for a Future Library." In *Proceedings of the Conference on Libraries and Automation held at Airlie Foundation ... 1963,* edited by Barbara E. Markuson. Washington, D.C.: Library of Congress, 1964.

52. Swanson, Don R. "Requirements Study for Future Catalogs." Final report to the National Science Foundation, grant GN 432, January 1972. Published in *Library Quarterly* 46 (July 1972): 302-15.

53. System Development Corporation. "Technology and Libraries." In *Libraries at Large,* edited by Douglas M. Knight and E. Shepley Nourse. New York: R. R. Bowker Co., 1969.

54. *UNISIST.* Synopsis of the feasibility study on a world science information system, United Nations Educational, Scientific and Cultural Organization, and the International Council on Scientific Unions. Paris: UNESCO, 1971.

55. U.S., Congress, Senate, Committee on Labor and Public Welfare. *National Library of Medicine: Report to Accompany S. 3430.* 84th Cong., 2d sess., 1956, S. Rept. 2071, pp. 5-6.

56. U.S., Court of Claims. Williams & Wilkins Co. v. United States, No. 73-68 (filed February 16, 1972). *Report of Commissioner to the Court.*

57. U.S., Office of Education. *Statistics on Land-Grant Colleges and Universities.* Washington, D.C.: Government Printing Office, 1946-70.

58. Weber, David C. "Working Paper on the Future of Library Automation at Stanford." [Stanford] University Libraries, 1971.

59. Withington, Frederic G. "The Next (and Last?) Generation." *Datamation* 18 (May 1972): 71-74.

ACKNOWLEDGMENTS

In the drafting of this report, I have been assisted by Mr. Stephen P. Harter, a Fellow in the Graduate Library School of the University of Chicago, who assembled and analyzed most of the economic trend data in Chapter 2 and was also of substantial assistance in the review of the major prior reports on libraries and technology in Chapter 1. Mrs. Julie Virgo and Mr. Charles Payne prepared the basic drafts of the material credited to them, in Chapter 6. Mr. Eric Halvorson assisted in locating some of the materials consulted and in checking the form and accuracy of many of the citations. Mrs. Ruth Meszaros and Miss Donna Gibson typed several prior drafts of the report; the final draft was typed by Miss Gerry Byrne; and the index was prepared by Mrs. Betty Grossman. I am grateful to all for their cheerful assistance.

Given the uncertain nature of the field, it seemed desirable to eliminate as many errors of fact as I could, and to try to ascertain, at least approximately, whether some of the more general conclusions I had reached seemed appropriate, or at least plausible, to other observers. This process of review, obviously limited in scope, was undertaken in two stages. A very small number of individuals were asked to read an early draft of the report in June 1972, prior to a further revision and submission to the Foundation in August 1972. Following submission of the report to the Foundation, and with the Foundation's concurrence, a somewhat larger number of colleagues were asked for comments and corrections. A variety of helpful comments were received in both instances. In several cases the responses reflected a substantial amount of time and effort. Those who aided in this process, and to whom I am indebted, include the following: Henriette Avram, Frederick Burkhardt, Robert Blackburn, Douglas Bryant, Fred C. Cole, Richard DeGennaro, William Dix, Warren J. Haas, Lawrence G. Livingston, Stephen A. McCarthy, John P. McDonald, Rob McGee, Carl F. J. Overhage, Charles Payne, Rutherford Rogers, Carl M. Spaulding, Basil Stuart-Stubbs, Don R. Swanson, and William J. Welsh. In addition, the principal investigators of the projects described in Chapter 6 were each asked to comment on the description of the investigator's own project.

Perhaps it is unnecessary, but propriety and custom lead me to add that despite the sage comments and advice my colleagues gave me, the responsibility for errors of judgment and fact are, of course, my own. Nor should I wish to imply that those who commented were necessarily in agreement with all of my conclusions or emphases.

I should also acknowledge my gratitude to Dr. Nils Wessell and Dr. James Turner of the Sloan Foundation, who arranged for a small grant-in-aid to the

University of Chicago to assist in the initial preparation of the report, who displayed remarkable forbearance when its preparation took significantly longer than had been estimated, and who arranged a small further grant to the University to support its publication.

INDEX

American Council of Learned Societies, 59
Annual Review of Information Science and Technology, 71
Association of Research Libraries, 15, 20, 43; Farmington Plan, 34
Atomic Energy Commission, 9
Automation and the Library of Congress, 1
Avram, Henriette, 72, 85

BALLOTS, 68
Ballou, Hubbard W., 45
Baumol, W . J., 14, 15, 18
Becker, Joseph, 1
Bibliographical control systems, 12, 27-31, 32, 75
Bibliographical data bases: need for, 6; standardization of, 6, 9, 27
Billingsley, Alice, 1
Blackburn, Robert, 85
Bowen, William G., 19
Bryant, Douglas, 85
Burkhardt, Frederick, 85
Bush, Vannevar, 51

Capital investment, 8
Carnegie Corporation, 39, 40
Catalogs, card, 22-23
Center for Research Libraries, 34, 38, 39, 40, 43
Chicago, University of, Library Systems, 53, 61, 69, 70
Clapp, Verner, 10
Coaxial cable, 47
Cole, Fred C., 85
Collections: growth rates, 33; limiting acquisitions, 35
Columbia University Libraries, 62
Computer-based file organization, problems of, 52
Computer-based systems: cost of, 52, 53, 54, 55, 60; criticism of, 52, 53, 60; evaluation of approaches, 58, 71, 79; long-term potentials, 56, 58-59, 78; regional library oriented, 60
Computer data processing, application of, 1, 31, 51, 57
Computer output microform (COM), 25, 32, 46, 61, 74, 77, 78
Computer software systems, 8
Conference Board Report on Information Technology (1972), 6, 8
Conference on Image Storage and Transmission (1970), 4
Conference on Interlibrary Communications and Information Networks (1971), 5

INDEX

Copyright: "fair use," 41, 48, 64; legislation, 4
Copyright act, United Kingdom, 49
Cost/effectiveness ratios, 2, 7, 8, 11, 12, 13, 74, 78
Council on Library Resources, 68, 71
Cuadra, Carlos, 1, 66

Data, machine-readable, 54; access centers, 21, 31
Data-processing systems, 55; on-line, 65; subsystems, 62
DeGennaro, Richard, 85
Discipline-oriented access systems, 9
Dix, William S., 18, 85
Dunn, Oliver C., 15, 16, 18

Economic values, 8
Economics of Academic Libraries, 14
Educational microwave networks, 48
Educational Resources Information Center (ERIC), 43
Electrostatic copying, 49, 77
Evolutionary change, 11, 14, 25, 31, 60, 79

Facsimile transmission, 47, 49
Fasana, Paul J., 62, 68
Federal responsibility, 3
Fiscal support, sharing of, 79

Government depository libraries, 4

Haas, Warren J., 85
Halvorson, Eric, 85
Harter, Stephen P., 85
Holography, 50

Information-access theories, 7
Information-literature-access systems, 8, 10, 73, 75
Information overload, 33
Information systems, analysis and planning, 5, 6
Interlibrary loan systems, 77
International Standard Book Numbers (ISBN), 25, 29, 30, 75
International Standard Serial Numbers (ISSN), 25, 29, 75
INTREX Conference, 2
INTREX data base, 67

Joint University Libraries, 34

Kemeny, John G., 6
King, Gilbert W., 1
King Committee, 2, 8

INDEX

Libraries: changes and improvements in, 3, 6, 7, 13, 14, 27, 32, 73-74, 79; expenditures and costs, 14-20, 21, 24; inflexibility of, 14, 22; physical plant, 20; potential crises, 24
Library Data Management System, 70, 71
Library of Congress, 1, 2, 8, 26, 55, 68, 72, 74; Airlie Conference, 2
Library operations, analysis of, 1, 4
Library-oriented systems, failures of, 57, 58
Library procedures, need for change, 9, 10
Library research and development, 3
Library Resources, Inc., 44
Library Services and Construction Act, 79
Library systems analyses, 9, 10
Licklider, J. C. R., 6, 10, 24
Literature, qualitative evaluation of, 32
Literature-access services, funding of, 4
Livingston, Lawrence G., 85
Louisiana Numerical Register Union Catalog, 30

McCarthy, Stephen A., 85
McDonald, John P., 85
McGee, Rob, 85
Man-machine interrelationships, 12
MARC II data, 28, 29
Massachusetts Institute of Technology, Project INTREX, 2, 67
Medical Library Assistance Act, 64
MEDLARS, 27, 57, 63, 64
MEDLINE, 63, 64
Microfiche, 43, 44
Microform system, shared resources, 3, 43
Microform technology, 41, 44, 45, 46, 49, 77; computer-controlled text, 5; problems of, 45-46; production and distribution, 42; use of, 25
Millet, John D., 18

National Academy of Engineering, 4
National Academy of Sciences, Committee on Scientific and Technical Communication, 4
National Advisory Commission on Libraries, 18
National bibliography, 3
National Cash Register, 44
National Endowment for the Humanities, 68, 71
National Lending Library for Science and Technology, 34, 38, 40
National Library of Medicine, 49, 63, 64
National library systems, development of, 1, 3, 8, 9
National Program for Acquisitions and Cataloging (LC-NPAC), 74
National referral network, 3
National Science Foundation, 62, 68, 71
National Technical Information Service (NTIS), 43

National Union Catalog, 3, 28
Networks: computer, 7; library, 5, 6, 9; information, 24
Northwestern University Library, 64

Ohio College Library Center (OCLC), 27, 29, 61, 65; costs of, 65, 66
Ohio State University on-line circulation system, 66
Operational systems, 9
Organizational mechanisms, absence of, 76
Overhage, Carl F. J., 67, 85

Paper, preservation of, 77
Payne, Charles T., 69, 85
Personnel, education and training of, 4, 5
Photocopying, 41, 42, 77
Photoelectronic composition devices, 61

Rand Corporation, 44
Regenstein Foundation, 71
Regional libraries and library systems, 3, 37, 60
Research fields, expansion in, 21
Research libraries, automation of, 2
Research materials, frequency of use, 23
Resources: imbalance in, 23, 29; modes of access, 22, 57; shared-access systems, 33-39, 76
Rockefeller Foundation, 40
Rogers, Rutherford, 85

Selective dissemination of information (SDI), 29
Spaulding, Carl, 44, 85
Stanford University Library, 53, 68
Stuart-Stubbs, Basil, 32, 85
Swanson, Don R., 2, 85
System Development Corporation, 3, 8, 76
System performance, evaluation of, 79
Systems of access, modification of, 13

Technical processing functions, 26-27
Technology, exploitation of, 2, 7, 9, 27, 28, 29
Telephone circuits, 47
Therrien, C. W., 67
Toronto, University of, 60
Transfer capabilities, 9, 60-61
Turner, James, 85

U.S. Office of Education, 68

Veaner, Allen, 62, 68
Video disks, 50
Virgo, Julie, 63, 85

Weber, David, 68
Welsh, William J., 85
Wessell, Nils, 85
Wigington, Ronald L., 5
Wigington Report (1971), 5, 8
Working Group on Network Needs and Development, 6

Xerox Corporation, 46